wVw
WALLKILL VALLEY WRITERS

Anthology 2015

SOUL GARDEN PRESS

MALDEN-ON-HUDSON, NEW YORK

Copyright © 2015 by Wallkill Valley Writers. All rights reserved.
Published in the United States by:
Soul Garden Press, P. O. Box 49, Malden-on-Hudson, NY 12453
Cover design: The Turning Mill, Palenville, NY
Front cover photography:
G. Steve Jordan, G. Steve Jordan Gallery, Water Street Market
10 Main Street, New Paltz, NY 12561
    Wallkill Valley Writers Anthology 2015
    ISBN: 978-0-9860936-3-0
    1. Literary Anthology 2. Hudson Valley Literature
Copyright Notice: All contributors to the *Wallkill Valley Writers Anthology 2015* retain sole rights and ownership to their respective works.

This volume is dedicated to writers, especially new practitioners of the art, who have important stories to tell, the courage to tell them and the discipline to make art using words.

TABLE OF CONTENTS

PREFACE ix

BYTHEMA BYRD BAGLEY 4
CLAUDIA BATTAGLIA 9
TIMOTHY BRENNAN 22
GLORIA CAVIGLIA 29
SUSAN CHUTE 37
GREG CORRELL 46
MEG DUNNE 55
BARBARA A. EDELMAN 63
KIM ELLIS 68
JEANNE-MARIE FLEMING 72
ALLISON B. FRIEDMAN 77
COLLEEN GERAGHTY 89
KATE HYMES 97
BARBARA TAYLOR MARTIN 104
LINDA MELICK 111
BARRY MENUEZ 116
ROSEMARIE NAVARRA 122
JENNIFER ROY 128

ACKNOWLEDGEMENTS 133
FOR MORE INFORMATION 134

PREFACE

The creative journey of **wVw** writers continues. Our mode of transportation has been our pens and laptops. We have traveled through time, memory and imagination to discover and explore new territories, stories, and forms. Writers who thought of themselves exclusively as writers of prose found poetry at the tip of their pens. Some writers, like myself, who did not believe we had a cohesive story to tell found ourselves writing evolving tales of characters whose ongoing saga is much anticipated by wVw writers. Others stepped onto terrain they had not inhabited in decades.

As an Amherst Writers and Artists workshop, wVw provides a safe and respectful writing space where writers may take risks, personally and artistically. We read newly written work in workshop and commit not to discuss it outside of our writing space. We critique the best of our work in manuscript sessions. The result is a collection of poems, stories and personal essays we just can't keep to ourselves.

wVw Anthlogy 2015 opens the door to our writing space and invites you to be our guest. Make yourself a cup of coffee, I prefer tea, wrap your hands around the warm cup and let its content take you on a journey: "I was happy to be leaving, grown up and leaving that God-forsaken place. That house where I was born, grew up, and love now, on that day it held now future n no promise, just futility, anger, hurt and pain." (Barbara Martin, *I Never Stop Seeing You There*); venture into a coal mine with a widow: "I want to know the darkness. My husband died in the mines a month ago, now. He was a shot firer. I just lost him to the earth. The men wouldn't let me see him. Just boxed him up and sent him back in the dirt." (Jennifer Roy, *A Cake for Pig Iron*); and sit alongside the grieving women of Greater Baptist Church who "after lemonade and dessert, they'd take out their crochet hooks and threads, and with fingers flying lay the deceased to rest again, with a review of the proceedings." (Bythema Bagley, *The Matriarchs of Greater Baptist Church*).

In November 2013 wVw lost a beloved writer and friend, Barbara Taylor Martin. Many came to love her and her stories, as much as we do, at the 2011 wVw Anthology public reading. We feel Barbara's presence: [we] "never stop seeing you there." Her words made us laugh, even when her stories were about growing up in 1950s Florida, a place with no future and no promise. In her poem *Three Elegies in November*, Susan Chute speaks for wVw writers: "I will remember your weight/ in the armchair beside me–/ the way you told stories/ as if at bedtime you were tucking me in."

Since our 2011 Anthology, wVw writers have been published in national and regional magazines and journals, and an award-winning anthology. Their writing has received recognition from New York state and Massachusetts literary organizations. wVw writers are frequent readers at regional and local venues.

Selections in this anthology include segments from longer works-in-progress. wVw looks forward to the publication of children's and young adult literature, novels, memoirs and poetry collections in the coming years. Once you have read these pieces we are sure you too will look forward to reading these writers once again.

Kate Hymes, Workshop Leader
Wallkill Valley Writers

wVw
WALLKILL VALLEY WRITERS

Anthology
2015

Bythema Byrd Bagley

BYTHEMA BYRD BAGLEY

The Divide

I live in a divided world of
those whose opinions matter
and those who will never have a clue.
The former, a small group, who
when the emotional volcano exploded,
spewing hot lava over everything dear to me—
the very essence of my being,
did not know what to say,
could not reassure me
they did not know the awful things going on.
They did not speak of the lies welded into a wall
that separated me from light, family,
those who meant me well. I suppose,
they meant well, yet did not have the courage
to warn me of the treachery I was blind to,
that plunged me into a deep cavern of despair.

The clueless and the evil ones, envied
what they thought was there, hoped that
one day it would all blow up in my face,
scald off the glow like acid splashed on soft skin
or maybe just burn enough to take away
what they perceived as an arrogance of self—
just too damned confident.

Well it happened,
mushroom cloud of despair,
spewed pain, confusion, doubt, fear
and other nameless things difficult to survive,
the two sides taking bets in the casino of life
as to whether I would survive. But, survive I did,
stronger than ever. There are new horizons now.
Damn them all!

The Matriarchs of Greater Baptist Church

It was late afternoon and we had just come back from Greater Baptist Church. It wasn't the usual Sunday service, but the funeral of cousin Grace's sibling whom we all called Sis. The church had been filled with vases of flowers, not from a florist, but choice blossoms from the many gardens in our little town. Miss Mary's pink and red peonies, Aunt Vivian's roses and Lillian's hydrangeas and delphinium, blue as the sky, were prominently displayed with daisies white and yellow. African daisies red and black filled baskets were placed, "Everywhere, there was a where," Aunt Sallie said. Growing one's own vegetables for nourishment and flowers for beauty was a mark of pride and respect in Fitz Henry.

The matriarchs of Greater Baptist Church, when they heard the news about Sis' passing, had baked the regulation coconut and pound cakes, apple and blueberry pies with wonderfully flaky crusts; they fried chicken and cooked greens for family and guests who gathered after the funeral to comment on the service.

"Well, she was put away nicely," Aunt Babe said, as she brought cool lemonade in frosted glasses for the women seated in the wicker rockers. This was a ritual I'd seen many times before. After lemonade and dessert, they took out their crochet hooks and threads, and with fingers flying, laid the deceased to rest again, with a review of the proceedings. There were recitations of the illness, family care and the minister's sermon for some time.

On this day, without warning, there was a clouding of the sky, a sharp wind and a short hard rain. The sky cleared suddenly, then the sun came out. Grandma said, "Well, Sis is telling us she's satisfied with the day." That was the signal for the ladies of Greater Baptist to put away their crochet hooks, say their good-byes and make their way to their respective homes.

༄

—**Bythema Byrd Bagley**, educator, administrator and musician, now explores communication and creativity through the artistry of the written word. In recognition of her career achievements in education, the arts and her contributions to community development, she has been awarded the Doctorate of Humane Letters by the Board of Trustees and the President of Delaware State University.

Claudia Battaglia

CLAUDIA BATTAGLIA

Riding the Beast

I am Juan Carlos and I am the man of the house since Papi left. My house in El Salvador is not like your houses. The walls are made of corrugated metal clipped together. Rows and rows of houses are connected, so if you knock into one too hard, they all fall down. We have only dirt roads, dust rising everywhere. There is no running water and sewage runs in the streets in rivulets, in hardened mud tracks made by passing buses. Most of the houses have dirt floors, and chickens and goats walk in and out. That's where I grew up.

Papi left for the U.S. when I was four years old. I am thirteen now. My Mami makes *pupusas* and sells them to the farm workers for twenty-five cents apiece. My two sisters and I are hungry all the time. There's nothing to do here, no work anywhere. We hang out in the street all day searching for scraps of food or just passing the time. A lot of the kids sniff glue; it helps them forget. I don't do that, but if I find a cigarette butt, I smoke it down to the filter.

I have to find a way to get some money. I see my Mami, her brow creased with pain and exhaustion, and I know I got to do something. She is only thirty-five, but she looks old. I promised her that I would buy her a house someday. Mami doesn't know it yet, but I'm getting ready to go to the U.S. People say you can earn a lot of money there. I know I will find work. I don't care what I do. I know I'm small for my age, but Juan Carlos, he knows how to work! Lots of people leave my village, *Usulatan*, and head north. Some find *coyotes*, the guides that bring them to the border where they can cross. But they cost $10,000. That's crazy.

Most young people ride *La Bestia*, the Beast. I have no money to pay a coyote. Anyway, they are mean bastards. They don't care about anything, only their money. If you are too weak to keep up with the rest of the group, they leave you there to die in the desert. Me, I'm a man now. I'm going to ride *La Bestia*. I've got it all planned out. Day after tomorrow, just before dawn, I'm going. I already wrote a note to explain to Mami. I know she'll be real sad, but honestly, I think she'll be happy to have one less mouth to feed.

When the day comes, I take two leftover *pupusas* and some water. I pack them, along with another pair of shorts, a pair of jeans, and two shirts in a *mochila* I stole from the market yesterday. I tuck the note into the cup Mami uses for her morning coffee, and I am off.

Just after dawn I arrive at the rail yard. The sun rests on the horizon as if deciding if it is going to rise today. I sit and wait for the long freight train. I am surprised at all the people waiting, maybe thirty. Some are younger than me; there are even a couple of girls. The morning is still cool. I feel nervous energy in the air. Boys are pushing, shoving, and laughing too loudly.

Finally an old man calls everyone around him. He explains the dangers of the trip. It is impossible to carry enough water to cross the desert, he tells us. Mexican police will throw you in jail, girls will be raped, and some will not make it alive. He asks us to think carefully before making a final decision. Then he asks who still wants to go. All hands go up.

"Okay," he says, "sometimes people come to the stations and give you a little water and maybe a mat to sleep on. *"Vayan con Dios."* And he is gone.

Suddenly we grow quiet and in a minute, I hear a low hum and I see the hazy shape of the long train snaking its way around the curve of the distant track. Soon the hum becomes a roar. I can hear nothing but *La Bestia*. My whole body is vibrating. Now she begins to slow down. Adrenaline is pumping through me. The whistle blows.

"Run alongside the train," someone yells. "Grab one of the ladders. The train doesn't stop, she just slows down."

"*Córale, córale,*" the screams come louder. As I run alongside the train, I heave my backpack up on the roof. Someone catches it. The train picks up speed again, so I have to run faster. From the rooftops of the train, I hear people shouting at me, "Run faster." My right hand grabs the railing, but slips off.

"This is it," I tell myself. With a final burst of energy, my feet pounding the ground, my breath coming hard, I bolt forward. And this time, I grab the bar, first with my right hand, then my left. My feet barely touch the ground. The train is going really fast now. Swoosh, I am airborne, my feet flying out perpendicular to the train.

"*Órale, órale Juan Carlos,*" I hear from above. I crunch up my legs and catch the last step of the ladder. I hang there for a minute to catch my breath. I need to rest. I am trembling from extreme exhaustion and exhilaration. There is another boy running beside the train, trying to grab my ladder, so I push myself up quickly and collapse on the rooftop. Everyone cheers. I look down ten or twelve feet to the ground and see only three kids are left behind. It is weird to see thirty people, some standing, some sitting, others lying down, all on the rooftops of the long serpent.

As the train picks up speed, the wind blows through my hair, now dripping in sweat. I know this is going to be a dangerous journey and I begin to understand the meaning of the words, *La Bestia*. But I have never felt more wildly alive than I do at this moment.

Soon we are in a more rural area. The trees on both sides of the tracks barely clear the rooftop of the train. We lie flat so the low branches don't knock us off, or cut us. The morning wears on and the noonday sun beats hot on my back. Even the wind is hot.

Hours and hours pass with nothing to do but hang on for dear life. Even lying flat, my back feels as if being whipped by the small branches. The roaring noise is deafening, so we can't talk at all. I don't know if it is the vibrations or all the excitement of the day, but gradually, I begin to feel numb all over, physically, and mentally. The nagging fears that had haunted me in the days before I left, are gone now. My only thought is to hang on. I am one with *La Bestia* and it soothes me.

The hours begin to blur together by late afternoon. I doze off for an hour or two; then the numbness is replaced by two driving needs, to eat and to pee. I finished my two *pupusas* and water hours ago. How much longer will the ride be?

"Papi made this trip. You can do it too," I tell myself. But as hunger, thirst, heat and exhaustion consume me, I begin to miss my Mami terribly. Did she cry for me? What did she tell my sisters?

All day I watch the sun make its journey across the sky and now, as it sits on the western horizon, the train finally slows down for the station at *Aguas Negras*. My body aches all over. I wonder if I will be able to stand. I am scared the police will catch me, but I have to pee. The train slows down in a series of lurches that almost knock me off. Many of the kids, who were laughing and joking when we left so long ago this morning, are crying. Some of them give up and get off here. I strain my eyes searching for anyone coming with food or water, but there is no one. I want to cry too.

It will probably be another twelve hours before we make another stop. Stiffly I climb down the ladder and pee behind the train. I could just wait here for the next train home, but home to what? If I go home, my future is clear. And besides, there is the promise I made to Mami. It is almost dark now. I am getting scared. I don't know what to do. Slowly, like an old man, I climb back up before the train starts again. I won't be alone. My hunger will accompany me to the next stop. Then I will decide whether to go on.

The Bandits' Noose

Dora walked cautiously into the bank in Mexico City. She scanned the room to make sure no one was observing her. There was a chill in morning air and the hazy grey smog had not yet burned off. Dora wore ragged and stained *huaraches*, a red and black knit *rebozo* that she drew tightly around her shoulders against the cool morning air of Mexico City, nearly a mile and a half high.

Miguel, slight for his fifteen years, came to her one morning last year, his *mochila* packed with a few things, and announced that he was leaving for the US. She knew all too well, the dangers that awaited him, and she knew she would miss him terribly. A clammy fear had gripped her that day.

But then, what could she offer him here? Drug cartels ruled the streets, in spite of the government's attempts to clean things up. The cartels had beheaded many city officials when they tried to crack down. Miguel's trip would only be dangerous for a week or two, nothing like the lifetime of daily danger he faced here as a teenage boy.

When Miguel left, he had promised to wire her money each month. She wondered if he would, but he had dutifully sent some money each month. At first, it was just a little. Now that he was settled, had a job earning five dollars an hour, he promised to send one hundred dollars when he could.

August was always a difficult month. Dora had to buy schoolbooks, supplies, and uniforms for Conchis, Yolanda, and Pequé. She had tried to save up for this expense, but even with one less child at home, it was not possible. The swine flu hit México hard this year, and little Pequé spent two days in the hospital. The bill was the equivalent of one hundred seventy-nine dollars, which to Dora was a ataggering amount. The hundred dollars Miguel wired her today was a small fortune to her. It would take her a month to earn what Miguel could earn in two twelve-hour days in the U.S.

Miguel told her to go to the Western Union office inside the bank, rather than the one near her house because it would be safer. She could pick up the cash and deposit it immediately into her bank account without setting foot outside. She had to stay focused now, as she stepped up to the bank window.

Too often, *bandilleros*, bandits, lurked around banks; they worked in groups of five or six, spreading out in the streets around the bank. A *bandillero* stationed near the front door would watch through special binocular glasses to see who withdrew money. He would phone the others; then the chase was on, though the victim was as yet unaware.

The *bandilleros* scattered around the bank's vicinity made a crude circle several blocks in circumference; quick calls back and forth tracked their victim's whereabouts as they gradually tightened the noose. Once at a safe distance from onlookers, there would be a flick of a knife, and if the victim was lucky, the *bandilleros* disappeared with the money in a split second, leaving their victim terrified and penniless, but unharmed. It was particularly dangerous for a woman on foot.

Aware of the impending dangers, Dora approached the window as cautiously and casually as she could, gave her pin number, three forms of ID, and answered the two security questions. When the bank teller returned with her money, Dora huddled closer to the window, swallowed up the five bills into the palm of her hand, tucking it beneath her *rebozo* and proceeded across the room to make her deposit. Once the transaction was completed, she drew in a slow, deep sigh; empty-handed, she headed for the door.

Outside, the brilliant morning air, while still cool, had warmed noticeably. She caught the first bus, which left her just twelve blocks from her house. All the while the bus bumped along the rutted streets, she held her hands in silent prayer, thanking the Virgin of Guadalupe. *Grácias* for guiding Miguel safely to Texas, *grácias* for helping him find a place to stay and a job. Most of all, she thanked the Virgin for giving her a son who was willing to work twelve hour days and send money home to his Mami instead of spending it on childish pleasures. Miguel was a good son.

Three houses before she reached home, she took out her key so she could quickly unlock the door, step in, and relock it. When she arrived home, she jiggled the key this way and that to release the rusty lock, and the door creaked open. Closing it behind her, she stood for a moment as her eyes adapted to the bleakness inside. Something was wrong. She pushed through the semi-darkness, fumbling for the light string, which hung down in the middle of the room. But there was no need. She could see that she had been hit. Everything had been stolen, her shabby furniture, TV, refrigerator, everything. The *bandilleros* had pulled up in a van and emptied the house in the short time she was gone. They must have been tracking her comings and goings. She had seen it happen to many others, but always thought she would be spared because she was too poor to have anything worth stealing.

She knew that neither her family nor the government could provide much help. Again she bowed in prayer, tears running down her face.

"Virgin of Guadalupe, I don't know how we will manage now. Sweet Virgin, *grácias* for guiding Miguel safely out of this terrible life. I dare to ask you one more little favor. *Por favor*, do not abandon us now in our hour of need. I have nowhere else to turn. I ask for your guidance and protection."

༄

Electric Fences

It's 11:30 at night. Arturo is just getting home from work. Roxie barks. I hear the key turn in the lock in the downstairs apartment of my house. The door closes. Water runs. My heart races, my breath tightening.

And there it is, like clockwork--ring, ring, ring. I pick up the phone. The monotone voice, exhausted, and depressed, comes to me in stereophonic sound, both through the receiver, and through the ceiling of the apartment below.

"Hi Arturo," I aim for a neutral tone.

"Did you just get home? I didn't hear you come in," I lie, wanting him to believe that I don't pay attention to his comings and goings, wishing to convey, through mental telepathy, perhaps, that he should not focus mine.

"Yeah," he answers flatly in his thick Spanish accent. A long pause.

"How was your day," I venture, wondering how much longer he can keep going on with so much work, so little else in his life.

"Very hard. Busy, very busy." Another long pause.

I hope he'll say he just wanted to say hello, then hang up. But he doesn't, leaving the responsibility of directing the conversation to me. In the pauses, I take careful measure of his mood. I know he is desperately lonely, though he never says so. He has no friends, no girlfriend. Last night when he called, he was on the verge of tears, saying he would commit suicide if he weren't such a coward. I didn't sign up for all of this. It is more than I am equipped to deal with.

"How did you sleep last night," I ask, worried about the weeks of sleepless nights, followed by twelve-hour days working as a dishwasher in a local restaurant.

"Sometimes," he responds. Did he understand the question? I switch to Spanish. Any conversation these days is tricky to navigate in English but in Spanish the difficulty is magnified.

"*Por qué no puedes dormir,*" I continue, "Why can't you sleep?"

"*Es su culpa,*" he says addressing me in the formal. "It's your fault," he replies, trying for a little joke. As in most jokes, I sense annoyance. "I want you to put up floodlights outside and a security system," he blurts out more like a demand than a suggestion.

We have had this conversation many times before. "I know you do, Arturo, but I don't want to," I say, happy that he is at the other end of the phone, and not in the same room as me, as he often was when he used to rent a room in the main house.

"But I worry about you when you take Roxie out late at night. I can't sleep because I worry about you like I used to worry about my grandmother in Guatemala."

"Did something happen to her?"

"No, because I make sure she is safe. In my country there are burglaries every day. Gangs patrol the neighborhoods as if they are the police. They know if you have pets. They keep track of your lights, your mail, your car, and they learn your schedule. My friend let her cat out one night. Two guys were hiding in the bushes by the door. As soon as she opened it, one grabbed the door and the other grabbed her. They raped her right in the yard, then robbed her house. That's why I can't sleep."

Arturo sleeps with a bat next to his bed. If he hears the slightest rustle of leaves, perhaps a passing deer in the night, he rushes out with his police flashlight in one hand and the bat in the other.

"I understand, Arturo. But a lot of your fear is because it is dangerous in your country. It is different here. I promise you it is safe here."

"Times are changing here too. It is not so safe anymore. Besides, you are getting older," he throws in, taking a shot at me, trying to weaken my position.

"I don't want you to worry about me."

"All the houses in my country have high fences with 440 volts of electricity around them. If anybody tries to break in, they get fried." He pauses to let this sink in, "Please just do this for me," he begs.

I want to tell him that it would be very expensive, and equally unnecessary, and that I do not want floodlights and a security system. I know from past conversations that we will lock horns and he will become even more single-minded in his attempts to pressure me. There is a long pause. I am lost in thought and don't know how to respond.

"Are you still there," he asks. "What about the floodlights?"

I no longer have the heart to tell him, "No," tonight, instead I say, wearily," I will think about it."

༄

—**Claudia Battaglia** is a retired teacher who has worked extensively with Hispanics, often undocumented. The dramatic and often tragic situations she has encountered over the years give her a unique view and compassion for their plight and inform much of her writing.

Timothy Brennan

TIMOTHY BRENNAN

Brooklyn Fragments
(a visit to Union & Nevins after thirty years)

sweat running
                before oil-on-glass
                        paintings   by Nick DeFriez—
                rooftop cityscapes
                    steel-wooled clouds
                    a bucket of tar tipped into a doorway—

across the gallery
                a woman's chin
                a man's eyes
                        I recognize from across
                        decades

near this former warehouse skulks
                      a boatscummed canal
trucks thunder the draw-bridge substructure

        moments of recognition follow   moments
      follow faces   changed
by the gap
        of years

                adult children converge evidence
intersections   in the lives of people we knew

I don't recall bird-sounds here
                         but gulls   but pigeons

                peeling stucco
                bricks' mortar-grooves grip
                                                roots
        of a shading ailanthus

we lived   we painted
                in the small manufactory next door—
        upholstery tacks caught in
                        cracks between floorboards

I caged the windows against rock-
throwers and thieves
                ran water   drains   lights   heat
                for our brick   steel   and terra cotta carapace

Italy of the vegetable gardens   fruit trees   old neighbors
gone
        corrugated garage doors
        and police locks
                        remain

        and across from   the South Brooklyn Casket Company
                      graffitied doorways

how hard and heavy the place bears now
                  into the hunch of my back
                                  and yet
how smoothly relaxed the young
                walk hand-in-hand under metal-halide lights
                          this hot Gowanus night
how cigarettes perfectly punctuate
                    their tattooed arms

                       ☙

The Urge

During revolution the walls collapsed— from mortar scraped away bit by bit, year after year, by children, now young adults, with metal scraps, with no particular desire to escape, but with a compulsion to see what lay beyond the stacked, cemented stones that bound their country. No adult's recollections sufficed to cure their curiosity, so every day for an hour or so on the way to school, where they were drilled in the creation myth, and the litany of historic battles and national heroes, they pulled contraband screwdrivers, or broken knives, or straightened bed springs from school bags to dig and scrape through mortar, like prisoners digging a tunnel. For hours adding up to days, then weeks to months, their hands grew calloused and strong from the work. Their eyes, however, weakened from squinting into dark crevices. As they grew, their passion contaminated younger siblings who also wanted to know what the walls kept from them, and who, with less patience, took to the streets to demand their demolition. They marched en masse, leaned and pushed against the walls. When the weakened joints gave and the walls crumbled, they were the ones with sight still strong enough to see what lay beyond it and who, though disappointed at how little difference there was between the world they knew and the one they had imagined, described with tenderness and enthusiasm any slight differences they discerned to their nearly-blinded older sisters and brothers.

☙

Young Enough in 1969

    the crab-crawl of wiper blades
    slows my car into
               snow blown sideways
    fuzzing the exit sign   past Syracuse
    on the vacant interstate
    tires slip in their own grooves   the wipers drag so

    I tilt my head outside to see
                this last view
    America's New York State   farmland   flattened
              before us heading west
    to Niagara's Rainbow Bridge

    feeling young is enough
                as all we know
    falls behind   as
    we go forward, saying   *Yes, we will*
                leave our parents' land
                            build different lives

    saying,   *Yes, I will*
                live outside this country though
    I fear   another young man
    may be selected   take my place
    bullet-scorched   mud-faced

we say, *Yes* to the peace we dream
as we plod through snow
and wind   now dark
Buffalo
to the border north
to Rainbow Bridge—

what the bullet-proof American agent
in his glass booth sees
when he sees us is me
saying *Hell, No* . . .
                when what
I'm saying to more than him
is *Yes*.

☙

—**Timothy Brennan** is a poet, painter and woodworker who has lived and worked in San Francisco, in Brooklyn, and now New Paltz, where he has been renovating his old house for over twenty years with no end in sight. His involvement with Kate Hymes's Wallkill Valley Writers group, has helped him to grow in his commitment to that often slow, difficult discipline through sharing work and guiding comments with serious and talented peers. His poems have been published in *The Chronogram, Awosting Alchemy*, and in the 2011 edition of the *Wallkill Valley Writers' Anthology*.

Gloria Caviglia

GLORIA CAVIGLIA

Viney's House

1

"You cannot go into the water for two hours after eating lunch," Mama said this daily after every meal at the beach house. Of course, I am well aware of why she said that. The adults relaxed after lunch, finished their wine, and took a nap. Drowning in the ocean may have been the reason they gave us; even as a child I knew better.

We were in Coney Island, at Viney's house. Viney was Mama's best friend, although they spoke to each other so harshly at times that it seemed they hated one another. Viney was a huge woman; she always wore a housecoat, the kind that snapped down the front. Hers didn't quite snap all the way down; it didn't fit around her thighs.

I saw her stockings rolled above her knees; her circulation must have been cut off by what looked like a thick rubber band around the tops. It bothered me to look at her legs, yet they fascinated me. Sometimes I couldn't stop looking. When Jigs noticed me staring, he said, "Hey, Mindi, you keep eating those sweet potatoes with butter, and you'll get them legs, too."

The thought of having Viney legs made me ill, but I didn't want to fuss about it because Mama'd be mad at me for making too much noise. Then Viney would pipe up, "Katie, you let that girl get away with murder. She needs the kind of discipline that the others had."

Viney had a big mouth. She was always telling someone what they could do, and where they could go. She didn't have a husband, her only means of income was the boarding house she ran year round, and where we stayed during the summer to escape the city heat. I thought it was unbearably hot there, but Mama said it was good for us to get the sea air.

Mama didn't go to the beach during the day. She liked to take a swim very early in the morning because "It is clean then," she said, "before too many people come and make it dirty." No one was allowed to go with her. That was her time alone, free to swim between the breakers and beyond, her cleansing swim. Then she'd come in from her swim, and begin her day with Viney.

Mama and Viney made coffee, the really black espresso kind. They pulled out from tins biscotti and taralle left-over from the night before. That was the kind of breakfasts I grew up on. No bacon and eggs, God forbid. And never milk. That was absolutely forbidden to touch their lips. We kids adopted their breakfast habits early on.

My sister, Anne, drank black coffee all day long and smoked cigarettes from the day she turned sixteen. Mama said she couldn't do much after we each turned sixteen; her parenting days were through. Mama told Anne she'd get the coffee nerves from drinking so much coffee, but she never listened. I didn't care for coffee. My four older sisters drank only tea, which I, too, preferred.

The boys drank wine, and of course whiskey when they could get it. My brothers, Mertz, who was hanging out after his first tour of duty sent him home with a surface shrapnel wound, and Jigs, who was hanging out for thirty days before his overseas assignment began, loved going to Viney's house. She had a cache of whiskey, and she drank and shared it in equal amounts. I couldn't believe how she kept up with them. Mama got upset when Viney gave Jigs more than she thought he should have. Jigs laughed, "Keep pouring, Viney, I'm buying." Viney did as she was told and kept pouring.

Mama told us girls to get on up to bed, tomorrow would be

another day. She didn't want us exposed to their drunken fancies, but I knew that there was more to it. I had done my own snooping in the beginning of July; I knew what was going on between Viney and Jigs, and had for several weeks.

After the fourth of July fireworks my sisters, Mama, Viney, and I went back to the kitchen for biscotti and taralle, and of course, black coffee. Viney poured whiskey into the coffee, and Mertz and Jigs drank as if they had been parched for days. Everyone laughed and talked at the same time, nothing new there, but I noticed Jigs touch Viney's shoulder. It was a momentary gesture, an intimacy between them, the kind of touch where no words are needed.

2

Jigs awoke to the chintz curtains blowing across his bed. He lay there for a moment watching them catch the side of the bed, and retreat back into the window sash with the breeze. It reminded him of the beach surf, in and out, in and out. He smiled, remembering last night. Good God, Viney could move for a big woman. He stretched himself full length on the metal-spring bed. He didn't care if the whole house had heard them last night as they rocked the old bed, the floorboards, and themselves, for that matter.

"I sure as hell danced last night," he whispered into the air, "Viney, may I have this dance? Again?" Jigs chuckled. He was always ready to dance any steps the ladies liked, and Viney loved to dance.

Jigs had to report August first for active duty. He had spent the last six weeks before coming to Viney's at Fort Dix. What a dump that was. It was a good thing that they had done all of that jitterbugging at the dance hall, because the army kept you on your toes from dawn to dusk and back again. Jigs had fared better than most; at five feet three inches with a wiry build and in good physical shape, he effortlessly went through the daily marching drills. And without a doubt, his nighttime activities helped his agility.

His brothers-in-law, Joe and Tony, were currently serving overseas. Tony was a sergeant in the 110th in France, and Joe was a seaman on a sub in God-knows-where. Jigs chose the Army because....well, just because. His mother almost suffered the stroke, the one she would have ten years later, when he told her he had enlisted, "Mama, it ain't gonna matter anyway," he reasoned with her, "I'd have been drafted before my birthday. This way it's no surprise".

"Jigs, please. I've got my hands full with your sister, Tess, due any day and her crying all the time for Joe, and your sister, Ann, smoking them cigarettes day and night and living on black coffee. You're killing your old mother."

"Aw Ma, I gotta do my duty. You know I'll be careful. I'll just dance 'round those land mines," he said with a smile and twinkling eyes.

3

Jigs groped and felt his way down the staircase of the boarding house in the dark, moonlight reflected in the dining room mirror, and lit his way into the kitchen. Jigs stubbed his toe anyway and cursed out loud. The clock hands were at 3:27 am. He sat on a kitchen stool, looked at his big toe beginning to show signs of swelling. "Damn it! And I've got a dance tomorrow evening."

"Oh, you do?" It was his big brother Mertz, who had heard him and followed him downstairs.

"Jesus! You scared me. Keep your voice down or you'll wake everyone up."

"Oh, you mean like you did a while ago with Viney?"

"Shut up, Mertz, you don't know…"

"I know plenty, Jigs. Don't think that Mama doesn't know or hear you two, either. What's wrong with you, anyways? She's, fat and three times your age. And she's Mama's friend. It would be in your best interest to cool this Viney thing right now." Jigs looked at Mertz and laughed. All he saw was jealousy.

Jigs could have any girl that he wanted, but he wanted Viney. Okay, so she was older. Just how much older no one really knew. She had been running this boarding house alone since they all could remember. Her fleshy thighs and upper arms disgusted most, but they turned Jigs on. Of course, he was well aware that Mama would kill him if she found out what he and Viney were doing, but Jigs could charm anyone with his smile and eyes, and even Mama would melt.

Mertz tried to be the papa of the family. And Papa, what the hell was his problem? He never came to the boarding house, and never, ever mentioned Viney or the trips Mama and the kids made ritually every July.

"Ah, Viney." Jigs knew that she would be sleeping like the dead now, her snoring quiet and steady. Since he had only come downstairs for a smoke and a nightcap, after his encounter with Mertz he grabbed the nightcap and headed back up to his own bed.

4

Jigs looked away from the window that he had been staring at for the last hour. She wasn't coming tonight, of that he was certain. He took a long drag off his cigarette, letting it sink into his esophagus and lungs for a second or two, then he slowly exhaled. The smoke engulfed him like fog rolling in from the sea. Jigs couldn't figure Viney out. During daylight she was all business at the boarding house, but when darkness came, she became his, all primal need and desire. His legs began to ache and the delicious pain travelled up his groin. Damn that woman.

Mertz had predicted that no good would come of his relationship with Viney. Damn Mertz to hell!

He probably was right. It wasn't an acceptable relationship to the outside world, but he was hooked. He needed Viney. She could do for him what all the bland women he knew couldn't do, or better, wouldn't do. He knew that Mama knew what was going on, yet she hadn't said a word to him. Confronting Mama frightened him as much as the thought of never being with Viney again.

He knew that Mama had heard them that night in the boarding house, when he and Viney had had a little too much whiskey. Mama looked away when Jigs and Viney made their way stumbling up the stairs to her rooms. Jigs saw a knowing look in her eyes the next morning as she served coffee to the boarders.

Jigs had kept a low profile ever since his discovery of Mama's knowledge and Mertz's warning to end it with Viney, "Christ, Jigs, what the hell's gotten into you? Can't you just date a regular woman?"

Viney was Mama's friend, Mama's age. Well, no one knew Viney's real age, but it was safe to say that she had seen the back end of forty. Maybe Mertz was right. End it now.

5

Viney couldn't believe that she had hoisted her large frame up the stairs to the attic above her private quarters. She needed to sit down, immediately; her legs couldn't hold her body upright a second longer. She plopped down on an old steamer trunk and let her eyes adjust to the afternoon light. She wouldn't allow herself to think about how she was going to descend; she would figure that out later. The driving need to come up here to spend some time with her past was a force so strong that she was unable to fight it. Katy and those damn boys of hers, especially that Jigs, were in her head way too often. She needed to think clearly, and coming up here in the dusty quiet was what she needed.

Viney stood up and opened the trunk. She pulled out a picture of Katy and herself, a framed black and white photograph, taken when they were teenagers. Viney smiled. She remembered that day so vividly. The photographer had come to Viney's house, and her mom, Lilly, moved a palm tree and a tall column from the hall into the parlor so the girls could pose by them. Viney and Katy felt so grown up in their long dresses with their hair ribbon-less.

Viney put the photo aside and pulled out hand-crocheted doilies in every imaginable size and pattern. The longer ones were used to put on sofa backs in the parlor, the shorter ones on the sofa arms. Viney pulled out a bed sheet with cotton lace crochet around the edges. She remembered it all too well. Her own mother had made it and given it to her for her trousseau when she had become engaged. Lilly had taken it out of the hope chest the morning of Viney's wedding to make up the marriage bed. Viney looked away at the memory. No use reminiscing about that, she decided, setting the sheet aside, and digging deeper into the chest.

She pulled out a small box with a scrolled J on the outside. She knew what was in it without opening it, a gold locket shaped like a coat of arms inlaid with three very tiny seeded stones. She and Katy were given the lockets upon turning eighteen. Somehow Viney ended up with the locket containing her own picture. Viney made a mental note to ask Katy if she still had hers; they should switch so each would have a picture of the other. She thought about that for a minute, then decided against it. Katy would question why she had been up in the attic in her condition, and Viney wasn't up to telling her the truth. At least not yet.

℘

— **Gloria Caviglia** believes that writing is like a massage for the soul. "This is the first time that I am being published with Wallkill Valley Writers. My work has been published in *Laughing Earth Lit*, and I have a non-fiction book being released for publication in 2014. I happily live and work in Dutchess County, New York."

Susan Chute

SUSAN CHUTE

Three Elegies: A Week in November, 2013

If suddenly you did not exist, Sallie,
who died at 8:30 on Monday,
I will remember how angry you were
when I showed up at your apartment
later than you thought seemly
after your special invitation
to pass the New Year's night awhile ago.
Wild-haired white-haired eighty-four-year old,
the Christmas cactus you gave me is about to bloom.
Swedish socialist in tattered clothes,
you still ride your battered bike by the banks
of the Hudson River from Christopher Street
downtown, down, down by the black river,
the sodium streetlights, the office windows—
stacked horizontal dashes across
the capitalist oligarchy you chided
in your cracked high voice—
the neon red cityscape
flashing in the water like wet slits
in your sightless eyes.

If suddenly you did not exist, Barbara,
who died sometime this Friday,
I will remember your weight
in the armchair beside me—
the way you read your stories

as if at bedtime you were tucking me in,
your animate inflections,
the eagerness from the back of your throat,
no matter the scene—gentle or gothic,
black or Sunday Church pastel—
my friend, you told your tale well.
You sit at the worktable yet
with paper and handmade book,
the dances of those glad eyes
behind your glasses disbanded.

If suddenly you did not exist, Doris,
who died this Sunday morning,
I will remember how I inhabited
your *African Stories* those forty years ago.
You stuffed my head with equal parts
passion and purpose.
Only with you could I claim my womanhood—
the argument, the element,
the solidity of you as another survivor
in the *Four-Gated City* where I would spend
a season of madness alone
in a locked room of my choosing—
and just when I thought I would dissolve
into particles of dust by the window light,
the door pulled open.
I would find I could open the door.

Now your hands, your words, your sights are stopped,
but the curve of all of you, rose-cheeked women,
is set in my blue-eyed stare yet to be stilled,
if suddenly.

Cento: Coming of Age in Pittsburgh

In Pittsburgh, beautiful filthy Pittsburgh,[1]
I'm disappearing.
Something
in me
is disappearing.[2]

Everything around me is crying to be gone.[3]

Dear train wreck, dear terrible engines, dear spilled freight,
    dear unbelievable mess, all these years later I think
    to write back. I was not who I am now.[4]

Hear the word of the Lord, ye children of Pittsburgh,[5]
while bombs fall from the sky
like dust brushed from the hands of a stupid god
and children whose parents named them will become dust…
and their tears will make a mud which will heal nothing.[6]

But going back toward childhood will not help.[7]
This dark is a major nation.[8]

In any random, sprawling, decomposing thing is the charming string
of its history—and what it will be next.[9]

I remember the first time I ever got drunk.[10]
We would try by any means
to reach the limits of ourselves, to reach beyond ourselves.[11]

A keen high nightlong cry
rises my silent, turning heart[12]
until all you are, Pittsburgh,
is a sleepless shimmer I will watch diminish down.[13]

Nevertheless the moon
Heightens the secret sleep long withheld
Dry for a rain of dreams—[14]

By redefining the morning,
we find a morning that comes just after darkness.[15]

Most mornings I would be more or less insane...
The news would pour out of various devices...
I would call my friends on other devices[16]
in the outcry from the kettle
that heats my coffee
each morning.[17]

Oh God of mercy, oh wild God[18]
Only Pittsburgh is more than Pittsburgh[19]

☙

[1] The Dancing by Gerald Stern. http://www.poets.org/viewmedia.php/prmMID/15437

[2] 619 by Kate Greenstreet. http://www.poets.org/viewmedia.php/prmMID/22460

[3] Walking in the Breakdown Lane by Louise Ehrdich. http://writersalmanac.publicradio.org/index.php?date=2013/06/21

[4] Epistle: Leaving by Kerrin McCadden. http://www.poets.org/viewmedia.php/prmMID/23598

[5] The Watchman of Ephraim by Paul Hoover. http://www.poetryfoundation.org/poetrymagazine/poem/241246

[6] Prayer for My Unborn Niece or Nephew by Ross Gay. http://www.poets.org/viewmedia.php/prmMID/22600

[7] Tear It Down by Jack Gilbert. http://www.poets.org/viewmedia.php/prmMID/19356

[8] It Is Difficult to Speak of the Night by Jack Gilbert. http://www.poetryfoundation.org/poetrymagazine/browse/105/4#!/20597199

[9] Distance and a Certain Light by May Swenson. *Collected Poems.* Langdon Hammer, ed. New York: Library of America, 2013.

[10] Driving and Drinking [North to Parowan Gap] by David Lee. http://www.poets.org/viewmedia.php/prmMID/16767

[11] Poem by Muriel Rukeyser. *The Collected Poems of Muriel Rukeyser.* 1st paperback ed. New York: McGraw Hill, 1982. p. 450-451.

[12] Nevertheless The Moon by Muriel Rukeyser. *The Collected Poems of Muriel Rukeyser.* 1st paperback ed. New York: McGraw Hill, 1982. p. 416.

[13] Pittsburgh by James Allen Hall. http://www.poets.org/viewmedia.php/prmMID/23596

[14] Nevertheless The Moon by Muriel Rukeyser. *The Collected Poems of Muriel Rukeyser.* 1st paperback ed. New York: McGraw Hill, 1982. p. 416.

[15] Tear It Down by Jack Gilbert. http://www.poets.org/viewmedia.php/prmMID/19356

[16] Poem by Muriel Rukeyser. *The Collected Poems of Muriel Rukeyser.* 1st paperback ed. New York: McGraw Hill, 1982. p. 450-451.

[17] Welcome Morning by Anne Sexton http://writersalmanac.publicradio.org/index.php? date=2013/06/22

[18] The Dancing by Gerald Stern. http://www.poets.org/viewmedia.php/prmMID/15437

[19] Tear It Down by Jack Gilbert. http://www.poets.org/viewmedia.php/prmMID/19356

How To Grow Old

Tell your story to whoever will listen
You might need some brownies
to corral your granddaughter
But tell your story
Talk about the old country
>How you wrung your laundry through
>the rollers above the shimmying washing machine
>then hung it out to dry

You might need some shots of Jameson
to lure your husband in
But tell your story
Talk about way back when
>Why you chased him from your bed,
>because you knew his seed would root
>in that too fertile field,
>then how would you get by?

You might need to talk over your whining daughter
Oh mom, we already heard that one
But tell your story
Talk about what happened then
>When you moved to the city
>to give her a chance to be someone more than you ever were,
>How your eyes fill up when she walks out the door
>in her frilly blouse and plaid pencil skirt

Yes tell that story   Go ahead
Ply your neighbor with coffee and fresh apple pie
fashioned from hands worn rough with oil soap and lye
Tell her your story
Talk about before and after
> *How your daughter lost her laugh*
> *the day her husband drowned and how he never deserved her*
> *since he divorced and if he could leave one woman*
> *he surely could leave another and leave her he did*
> *though not the way you expected, you'll grant him that*
> *And not only doesn't she laugh,*
> *she also doesn't cry*

Yes say it
Let the words pour forth from your hell-bound heart
because you committed that unforgivable sin when
you were young and easy and free and tell them
Talk about bargains, say look
> *You raised two angels for daughters,*
> *you can't help it if they ended up with sorry specimens for men*
> *It could not mean you won't meet them again in the end*
> *now could it?*

And there's still more to say
But no one hears as you scream from your hospital bed
by the dining room window above the garden where
the dahlia bulbs were not brought in and now will never bloom again
No matter, you'll try once more, you'll blurt it out

But there's your granddaughter with the ice blue eyes of her father
that madman you could never stand, and she's reading you poems
from one of those piles of books by the stairs
And okay now
her voice is softly rising and falling and you think
if that's what she wants to do, well you guess it's fine with you

You've grown old.
Your story is told.

༒

—**Susan Chute** is a librarian who moved to New Paltz from New York City a few years ago. At The New York Public Library, she co-taught a poetry/art workshop called *The Colored Line, The Pictured Word*. When she's not reading & writing, she spends her time learning and archiving at Women's Studio Workshop and giving tours at Lincoln Center. She is grateful to Kate Hymes and Wallkill Valley Writers for building her a community of craft and friendship.

Greg Correll

GREG CORRELL

The Music of These Fears

Light wants in. It sneaks through bent blinds to find Nana's picture glass, small bottles, and me. Bright rainbows dot the wall. I finger eye sand and wriggle out from under her bed, peek over: big brother Chris thumps his knee, grunts; baby brother Kirk curls tight on the far side. I lay my cheek on wrinkled sheets and hold my breath, my heart-beat in my ears.

The wind-up alarm ticks down to wake-up time. I make the sounds into word-pictures, see letters dance: t-tuk t-thuk t-tuk t-thuk. I rub bare feet together; big toe grips big toe and I feel smooth, all the way up.

I crawl into the bathroom and close the door. I sit to pee, chin on fists, elbows on knees, and whisper words, turn them which-ways in my mouth: jam-bo-REE…ju-bi-lee. I see dic-tion-ary syl-la-bles, like Nana showed me. I make pretend squares with my foot, and see syl-la-bles.

How does Nana sleep in a chair? My lips go in and out: up-PAH—up-PAhhhhallnight

I sit up, lean on a stiff arm, look in the bowl. I flip my elbow in and out, teeter-totter side-to-side. I sit back, stare at cracks between pink tiles 'til I can't blink—pink dies, turns green—and see word-pictures, the story of last night; I see

Crazy Eights 'n Slapjack, Wonder Bread burgers, Have Gun, Will Travel, cream soda floats, m-lum…splash-y bath, sticky-damp PJs, up way past bedtime—so what! bouncebounce catty-wampus, wrestle, make a pyramid, fall over…big sister Dana waves fingers over us—do it, pinch-tickle!—giggle-fart crazy, crack-jaw nuts…

Nana: "Boys! Neighbors!" Dana: "Shush!"—we shush back—I dive under the sheet, point-y toe squeal!

Chris: "Oh. I'll just SIT on this mountain"—bounces—SQUEAL! I think at him: Do it again! He DOES.

Kirk: "Metoometoo!"

Careful: Kirk climbs on, we slow down; no roughhouse, no crush or smother, flip or throw, with his heart condition and all…

I see his heart, and black lines like snakes—I push it away…

Poke-poke, under-over covers; still too wild!

Dana takes Kirk out to the big chair—we sit up: no fair!

Chris, chin out: "Don't watch TV, Kirk!"

Nana: "Lie down now"—squirm in, chins above sheets; Chris, straight arm, a judo chop: HIS part of the bed. She settles over us to read One Fish, Two Fish.

Chris: "No, it's a baby book." He reads with her anyway. I close my eyes, see each word; he smacks me when I swim.

She closes the book—sweet kisses—and turns off the lamp. "So, go to sleep now, boys."

Kicks, under the sheet. His arm sneaks to tickle my neck; uh-oh, my pillow book, The Best of H. T. Webster. Tug-of-war; he wins…

"You can't have Nana's books in bed."

What? nyuh-uh, no such rule! I kick him; that does it: "You stop!"—kick, you stop—kick, "YOU!"—kick, you!

Dana: "I'll tell Mo-om!"

—gotcha-last his foot; he rolls over, ignores me, to make me sleep.

Blue TV flickers through the door crack; grown-up shows: a doctor's a killer, a woman has a sick brain; I count words on fingers. Chris sleeps.

"Tune in Next Week! on…"

Dana carries in sleepy Kirk, tucks him in with us. She and Nana take turns, in and out of the bathroom. I watch through eyelashes.

Eyes open. I bend over, fingers on wall, floor. The sun is higher; Sunday scary crawls my tummy—NO. I sit up, close my eyes tight; I see

…lights off; Dana-talk, Nana-whispers…I make finger-letter words, add pictures: a bee for be, an eye for I…I find a story: bumble-bee high in the sky, wants to be a bird; sonic-boom NO… bumble-bee falls…

The clock in the dark: t-thik t-thuk. Quiet. Snores.

Out of the covers slow—squeeze nose, stop sneeze—shiver… slide under the bed, feel for the flashlight, for The Best of Punch, hidden cartoons…shoulder to one ear, hand covers the other; squinch-face, push the metal switch—cliCK! 'n red fingers over yellow light.

Springs squeak…wait…still asleep?

I open the book, flip pages. Some are funny; most make no sense: a giant machine with a zillion parts? makes road lines, paints them wrong?

I close it, push it out, follow. Hands 'n knees to her green shelf; pull one, squint: no; pull, squint: NO; pull: YES! mask on cover: Greek Myths. Nana reads this! Crawl back, slide under, arm out, pull it in. I turn—bony macaronis scrape springs—flashlight: shake-shake—wait: listen…

I put fingers on syl-la-bles make sounds, like she showed me; Thee-see-us; Chuh-ROW-nose—sounds wrong; Kai-clops—one-eye monster; Oddy-see-us—sounds wrong; A-the-na—owls; App-ol-lo—Appollo! sun man, sun rays…

Flashlight! shake-shake: tiny wire glows gold. It's really Chris's…he'll hit me, 'n for good reason…

I use up the last light; I wake up, the Gods in my arms, Apollo's ray-gun rays…

Eyes open, legs gone to sleep. I hop off the seat, put fingers on the rusty-shiny flusher—no: too loud. I stand on toes, turn on a squee of water; pipes rattle and clang—too loud—in her spider basement.

Clang stops. Water runs. Soap-soap. Finger foam. Soap-soap. Finger wrinkles.

I climb on the tub rim to watch my face in the mirror, 'n fiddle fingers clean under the faucet. I make grenade explosion faces, horrible blown-up faces. I crank the water off with both hands; loud unk-unk 'n after-bangs, down in those pipes.

I shake no 'n nod yes at mirror me, lean in on faucet handles, slip a little—how'd my feet get wet?—put forehead to cool glass; eye-to-eye, I try to recognize myself.

I squeeze my tummy: school this year. Big boy. I roll my forehead on glass, pull mouth down 'n eyes wide, from the top: WAY scared.

I climb down, listen: nothing? tiptoe out, to the bedroom door, listen: nothing? I turn the knob with both hands, pull, bend to look through the crack under the hinge: books. I bend the other way, see Nana in her fat chair: head back, blanket tucked, feet out; books, newspapers, magazines. Daylight behind her, through porch-door curtains.

I pull the knob, slip through. Right-hand: her clean white kitchen. Left-hand: Dana snores on the roll-a-way, behind the lion-claw table, a pillow over her head.

Dust dots float in sideways light, wink off 'n on…I watch one float…rise…fall…

Nana tilts her head, looks me in the eye, says, "Hi, sweetie. I guess I'm just being lazy."

Hands up. I surrender. She smiles. I growl.

Her long, vein-y fingers circle her sunk-in eyes. "I have to make us breakfast." She puts palm to temple, rubs her headaches; curls a fist 'n pushes against her thin face, her cheek, jaw, neck.

My elbows bang my ears; claw hands in the air, I slow-spin past her, stiff-leg hunchback tippy-toe. I look back, under my arm: she pushes long hair into a gray pile, bobby pins in her teeth. She asks me something.

…monsters don't understand…

She straightens papers and magazines on the sofa, stacks her books on the end table; dust dots rise. I land at her book shelves, paw at nature books; hook and pull out three. Cheeks between knees, shoulders scrunched, I stack by size: big "Audubon," then "Powell's Trip Down the Colorado." The little "Golden Guide to Rocks and Minerals" on top. Chewed newspaper strings stick to my favorite pages.

I fill my eyes with quartz and jasper, opal and mica. Tap-tap hairs, on the back of my neck; I like to turn pages. I cover names, to guess; I like remembering. I cheat a lot. I can't syl-la-ble some, the letters don't look right: g-ne-iss?

I close Rocks. Sun pops a tree-top; dust dots glow. Nana feels around for her big glasses, and sighs when she puts them on. I sneak looks sideways, watch, wait—she rises, walks by; I sit up, lean back, and she runs her velvet-y hand over my crew-cut. "Urrr," I growl.

⁂

Spinning in Itchgrass

Freeze tag's too slow and breathless chase is not enough: I need spin.

Fingers on home-base maple tree, palm on knee, ratchet gasps—I catch copper-bang breath—rev-rev—circle the tree—fingers iddl-iddliddle on bark—run upright—let go 'n arms out 'n SPIN— grass hedge tree roof tree cloud roof tree roof—Stacey Sally Steven David Phillip Chris race around me go match-head blurs go firefly lines go invisible go watch out! dizzy hey! go unfreezable—

    sort-of try not to go hit anyone faster inside speed turn turn cheeks jiggle mo(huh) ment(huh) hum(huh)—go brave nerve spin scary swerve now now now—

    turn world without words spin no talk no listen go no wrong no trouble go no wait go demented top go Tasmanian angel eyes roll up go drill the floor of heaven and

    fall in itch-grass earth under me boiling green turns I fall my brain says fall waxy green stain grind turn I am magnetic north turn can't get ahead of turn surrender to dizzy 'n sickdizzy itchgrass splendor—

    sweet bugs crawl the crush of me under me go climb my white tee swarm ankles, forearms roll sorties behind knees antennae in scout shorts turn un-reachable scrabbles, up my back turn might even be real—

    I don't care! part bug, part Titan; I make the Earth spin, wake Vulcan in his cave; his extinguish his forge, steal his hammer; I'm Chaos, crazy-wild child of evil Chronos, the boy who stops infernal machines—

    "Blame it on the Bossa Nova" th-thumps at forty-five rpm; I squint to see sky turn after-dinner blue through sweat-blur lashes turn pluck grass as the globe tips, sick—delicious—I hear bicycle bells—

Yells! in my face; kicks! at my foot; I see myself from sky above...

in a yard on a street, near shores of blue-green wheat, bristle-brush corn, velocipede Kansas rolls in all directions...I zoom to fields beyond dead-end Eby, full of striped blue racers, slow boy garters; aqua-shell craw-daddies, in a million mud holes; lazy Ozark box turtles, cottonwood redoubts, perimeter woods...still I spin under caravel clouds, torn from rocky-tops way out west

I lose true north...

all compass points are fare-thee-well, beyond the rim, the upturned bowl, the forever curve, of plain old Kansas...thick hides un-seen wonder, eclipses The Big Book of Marvels, My Weekly Reader, all encyclopedias and brave adventure stories...

not for you, murmurs flat horizon...

I grip the grass, tear out handfuls. Yes! turn It is! turn I will dig my way out, past the far-a-way edge, peel back the sea of thatch, split black earth 'n fathoms of tenta-cle'd turf, up-root it all—

A meadow-lark sings. I hear cree-kets in the grass, kid-screams in the yard, moth-flutter in porch light—Stacey leans over me, hands on knees, pants—"Are you playing yet?" I roll eyes to her, smile, shake No—still too dizzy, too turn-turn inside-out—she glances back, shrieks! trips on my leg, runs; skids a right-turn 'round the safety tree—

I say yes.

Chris, close behind her, tries to tag me with his freezer foot; I move and he misses by inches; I shout the lie: "Frozen!"

Play talk: "Can't hug base!" "Got you!" "Quick, unfreeze me! touch me!" "One Mississippi..."

My Jon Gnagy paint set spills in the sky: crimson, yellow ochre, azure, Prussian blue. Plum. Meridian green, dark purple sky; light dissolves in flares of red-orange, touch silhouette cypress, snarl'd sycamore; stars wink in the ultramarine east…soon we'll get the "Come along," "Okay, inside," "Boys?" the foot stamps "I know you can hear me," "Inside! Right now!" the screen slams 'n steps outside "I mean it! Boys?" and a final bee; I blink, swat—

o one more burst of speed, one more war-whoop, one more breathless escape

I say Yes.

The world slows—I never quite finish a final inside turn. I roll over, uproot a long blade, for between my teeth: buccaneer knife. The new streetlight b'zizzitzs, flickers, snaps off; everyone stops—"time out!"—parents, too, to watch—

I turn to look across the street, into our dark garage…

Dad. Head up, or down? back bent, or straight? fists, or flat hands?

Sea-green light comes all the way on; am overhead POP—cheers and hoots; Chris runs down distracted Kaisers—"I got youuuu!"—a car revs on 83rd; I hold up my hands, move minty arcs of street light between plum-black fingers—

Dad? I peek: he went inside. Too many neighbors.

"SO? Are you playing yet, or what?" Stacey pushes my bare toe with hers.

Her smile makes my stomach tight. I sit up, my mouth shapes sound:

"Yes."

☙

—**Greg Correll** is finishing a book with his daughter Molly. He's had two plays staged, one at the Makor in New York City. His poetry has appeared in two anthologies. He's written for Salon and The Good Men Project. He was chief engineer of Yale's Climate Institute collaboration site, won a Clio for Best Packaging, and illustrated for *The New Yorker*.

Meg Dunne

MEG DUNNE

Right Side of the Tracks

I am seduced by the hypnotic rhythm of metal against metal, distant and faint at first, methodically pulsating to a climatic crescendo, accompanied by a whistle blowing. I travel back to childhood, to a town divided physically and psychologically by the Main Line of the Erie Lackawanna Railroad, a town whose very existence relied on the American Brake Shoe Company, whose workers, backs bent over molten iron as their lungs filled with deadly metal dust, toiled in the foundry's fiery inferno.

In the early twentieth century, Poles, Slavs, Ukrainians, Hungarians and Russians fled oppression and famine in distant lands, and came to a small New Jersey town by the hundreds to work the foundry. Like the people of color who they found themselves living and working alongside, these Eastern European immigrants discovered how the American dream could resemble an American nightmare. My mother remembers the 1920's; the KKK burning crosses high on the mountain as a message for the people of color and the newly arrived Catholic immigrants. This was not the Deep South; this happened in my hometown in northern New Jersey less than a century ago.

The Main Line of the Erie Lackawanna reinforced the divide of race, class, and ethnicity that defined our small town for the generations. Four sets of cold hard immovable steel track. On the East Side, the right side of the tracks, lived the prosperous: the foundry owner, the doctors, the lawyers, and bankers who left their homes on the hill every morning dressed in suits to commute on the Main Line to NYC. They never had to cross over to the other side of the tracks.

The people who lived on the West Side, the wrong side, particularly the women, were not so fortunate. The women, who worked as housekeepers, cooks, nannies, and seamstresses to the wealthy, had to cross the tracks to get to their jobs where their labor and skills were needed but their presence wasn't wanted. Just crossing the tracks to go to the post office meant the risk of being called racial and ethnic slurs, and the possibility of getting hit by thrown rocks if you didn't leave quickly enough.

The foundry belched toxic fumes and soot onto the West Side of town, the wrong side of the tracks. The fumes and soot eventually took many a life, including both my grandfathers. Generations of foundry men worked hard, prayed hard and drank hard. They sought solace in both the Catholic Church and the many bars near the foundry.

Outside the foundry's main gate was the company store, the only store where the immigrants could purchase the necessities they couldn't grow or make for themselves: the rare pair of shoes bought only when there weren't any hand-me-downs left to go around, medicine when the folk remedies no longer worked, cooking oil, flour for baking -- even the sacks were put to use and sewn into clothes. Despite working long twelve to fourteen hour days in the heat and smoke of the foundry, the paychecks barely sustained these hard working immigrants. The company store charged high prices while extending credit that perpetuated endless debt for the workers' families.

In the early 1950's my father, proud and stubborn, bought a house on the right side of the tracks, one of the first Polish Americans to do so. Being Polish and Catholic he had two strikes against him, and my parents endured threats and intimidation. The women of the neighborhood organized tea parties to strategize how to prevent my family from moving in. These neighbors encouraged and supported a family to remain in the house my parents purchased for more than a year before moving out, but not before vandalizing the house my parents had worked so hard to buy.

Once my parents, with two young children, ages five and one, were able to move in, they had to contend with neighbors on each side trespassing and claiming my parents' property as their own. One time a woman on the street came out of her house and knocked my brother off his tricycle yelling for him to go back to his end of the street. While the neighbors were unsuccessful in their attempts at intimidation, it took fifteen years before any of the immediate neighbors would acknowledge my family.

I grew up in the late 1960's through mid-1970s, as the Main Line was reduced from four to two sets of steel track. The foundry's days were numbered; yet the smokestacks still belched rust-colored soot, covering everything downwind with toxic metal dust. I watched men tend the fiery furnaces on the catwalks high above the train tracks below.

Sixty years after my great grandparents arrived in this town, I was ridiculed and bullied for the ski at the end of my name. Old time neighbors hadn't forgotten their unsuccessful attempt with their tea parties to keep my family from moving in. Upon returning from Vietnam, my brother was flat out told by the head of the town's water department, a neighbor, that he would not hire a "Pollock."

Childhood memories of a town divided physically and psychologically by the Main Line of the Erie Lackawanna Railroad. The hypnotic rhythm of metal against metal, receding into the distance, the sound of a whistle blowing its haunting melody, transport me to a time, a place inhabited by memory's ghost.

☙

Cusper

Cusp: A point or time when an individual is poised between two states-of-being.

I am a Cusper. Not truly a child of the 1960's; a Boomer I am not, nor does the Gen X-er label fit. I came of age in the mid-1970's when the optimism and idealism of 1960's youth was but a memory, nostalgia, old protest songs on the radio. Civil rights, women's equality, social justice, already becoming ideals of a past, a past I shared -- just barely.

Stark memories in black and white burned into my memory as I sat on the living room floor watching a black and white TV: a plane carrying the casket of the president back to Washington D.C., then of a boy and girl standing next to their mother numbed in grief as a team of horses pulled the casket containing our president, their father, her husband. JFK's funeral became my first memory of death. My mother insisted I watch the black and white TV. It was history, and as an American, my duty was to watch and bear witness. Not quite four years old, I watched, live on TV, as Lee Harvey Oswald was shot. These images of death, murder and grief would not be the last black and white images burned into my memory.

As a young child in the 1960's I heard the music of peace, love and protest, but even then I sensed a disconnect. Every night I watched that black and white TV, and saw people marching for civil rights, protesting the Vietnam War. They were confronted with hatred and brutality. I saw the assassinations of Malcolm X in 1965. In 1968, I witnessed Martin Luther King Jr. gunned down on a hotel balcony. A few months later, Robert Kennedy lay in a pool of blood on a restaurant floor dying from his wounds.

Upstairs in my bedroom I had peace beads, peace signs, and happy faces, in all the day glow colors of the time. But every night downstairs in the living room I watched soldiers fight and die in Vietnam. When I was ten my brother went off to fight in Vietnam; he was lucky he came home alive and in living color, not in a box as a neighborhood boy did. As the 1960's ended I watched men walk on the moon and the concert at Woodstock in black and white on the old TV. Images burned into memory, in black and white, from the old TV. Then the world and a generation changed color.

Never again would a generation of youth believe the ideal that change is possible with such naïve conviction. The 1970s our nation, the world and a generation was on the cusp of change. The groundwork of cynicism was being laid for the Gen-X-ers who followed the boomers. Never would I experience the optimism of the boomers' youth, but never could I embrace the cynicism of Generation X.

Too young, too old, never just right, I long ago quit searching for a tribe of my own. I am an American Cusper.

ೞ

Life Song (Magicadia)

I watched them emerge into night's blackness
White as the moon with huge red eyes
I felt their moist, newly-formed wings that when fully dry
Reveal a pattern so beautiful that cathedral stain glass cannot rival

Magicadia cicadas
Seventeen years they waited for this moment
For these four weeks
Their last weeks of a long life
To sing
To sing their Life Song

For weeks they have been my constant companions
Beginning as a hum in the distant wood
Barely audible
My soul stirs
The fourth seventeen cycle of my lifetime

Only two in 1962, I have no memory of their song
June of 1979 my life in turmoil
I could not hear their chorus
1996, I began to unearth
What lay beneath the surface of my heart and mind
Faint rhythms of my Life Song
Again I did not hear the passionate
Life Song surrounding me by the millions

2013 a new millennium
I am discovering
My Life Song
I have been waiting and I am ready
This fourth, seventeen-year cycle
I am ready to listen and
Sing with them
For now I know they are part of
The Life Song
I will sing

☙

 —**Meg Dunne** is an environmental scientist, visual artist and writer passionate about nature and animal welfare. She and her husband, with their three rescued pit-bulls, live, create and dream in the mountains and woods of the Hudson Valley.

Barbara A. Edelman

BARBARA A. EDELMAN

Forever Dorky

I. Musical Comedy

For three months in 1970, or maybe it was 1971, I was a student of the accordion. I carried my rented accordion in a bulky, square case that looked like a ventriloquist's dummy-carrying case. Accordions and ventriloquists – I was a frizzy-haired, brace-faced, ten-year-old, walking vaudeville act in search of a spotlight.

A year or so after the Woodstock festival shook the country, I walked three blocks from my house to the large, beautiful, early 20th-century house of Mr. and Mrs. Borgia for twice-weekly accordion lessons. Mr. Borgia had taught the clarinet to my sister, and Mrs. Borgia taught many instruments, including the accordion. I loved the Borgia home. It was a center-hall colonial with a glassed-in vestibule that contained velvet cushion-covered seats and wrought iron coat trees. I would have liked to bring a favorite book to this vestibule, taken a seat on a velvet cushion, and enjoyed a quiet hour or two of reading, especially since my favorite books at the time often featured girls sitting on velvet- covered seats reading books.

Mrs. Borgia greeted me at the door and ushered me into a sort of music room-library combo space: one of the many spacious, high-ceilinged downstairs rooms in her house. I heard distant sounds of string, possibly woodwind instruments from unseen students of Mr. Borgia's. The house was so large that there may well have been a half dozen music rooms.

A faint smell of dinner often lingered in the air. It usually smelled good, and I half hoped Mrs. Borgia would offer me a plate of leftovers rather than watch me strap on that moronic instrument and then draw my attention to the bars of music that were no easier for me to read this week than they had been last week.

The accordion is an interesting combination of silly to look at, sillier to hoist onto one's not-yet-developed chest, and quite difficult to master. It combines the less attractive elements of piano keys, woodwind keys, and fireplace bellows, requiring coordination far beyond that of this playground and gym class spaz.

In later years, I'd watch accordion players on TV as comic figures, such as the annoying wedding entertainer or has-been vaudevillian, and I would cringe; what the hell had I been thinking? Probably that it wasn't even remotely like the flute, clarinet, piccolo, or guitar, all of which my sister played well.

Recently, however, I've noticed a trend of young women in their twenties playing in klezmer, zydeco, and bluegrass ensembles. And what are they playing? The goddamn accordion, that's what. And they're cute and sexy – lots of skimpy but cute flowery sundress and Western boot ensembles – and don't appear anything remotely like has-been vaudevillians. Clearly, I missed the boat on this one. I shared this possibility with my mother not too long ago.

"You could have been famous if you'd stuck with it," my mother said firmly. "But you dropped it, just like you dropped everything. Violin, modern dance, tennis, coin collecting."

"Coin collecting doesn't belong on that list," I said. "I never would have achieved fame and fortune from collecting coins I bought by the dozen for one dollar at the hobby shop. And regarding violin, tennis and modern dance, let's just say I know my limitations."

II. Horror

Flash Gordon was there in silver underwear. I wore jeans. Among my happiest teenage memories – there were three, maybe four – were excursions to midnight showings of Rocky Horror Picture Show in 1977 and 1978.

Twice, I saw it at the Waverly, the Greenwich Village theater, where the witty and sharp audience participation phenomenon was born. Plus that was where I saw my first drag queens. But making the midnight scene in New York City was tough for a bunch of suburban kids. Money had to be spent, parents had to be lied to, so we traded some wit, sharpness, and drag queens for convenience.

Most often, we went to the Town 2 Cinema in New Rochelle to get our Rocky Horror fix. It was local, convenient and most of all, efficient, in that one's number of viewings of Rocky Horror were key; the closer the theater, the more frequent the viewings. Sixteen was my total by high school graduation.

I saw it twice in Queens in the early 1980s, but I do not count those viewings in my total. The pop culture references had changed by 1983, and frankly I didn't want exotic outer-borough residents becoming part of the wallpaper of my teen touchstone.

Jeans, along with a t-shirt, was my preferred style profile when viewing Rocky Horror at the New Rochelle Town 2. I looked generic. Once I half-heartedly dressed as a Rocky Horror character: Magenta, the frizzy-haired, bisexual, incestuous housemaid. (I chose Magenta because I already had the hair for it.) The smoky eye makeup, false eyelashes, purple-red lipstick, short-skirted and torn French maid uniform, fishnet stockings, and black boots sat on me with about the same degree of élan as would roller skates on a beagle.

As luck would have it, the night I chose to look like a cross dresser's nightmare was also the night that the Grateful Dead documentary opened on the second screen of the Town 2 (hence the 2) at midnight. All the suburban hippies who were way too cool for the bubblegum, porno-pop /punk soundtrack of Rocky Horror were out in force for the Dead. It didn't matter to me that the three or four people I was with looked equally ridiculous; they didn't care, and I did.

A certain suburban hippie I knew fairly well was on line for Dead tickets. Her name was Meg and she was escorted by two guys she was sleeping with. "Purely platonically," she insisted. Meg smoked Newport Light (box) cigarettes in a plastic cigarette holder with a tortoise-shell patterned filter. Yes, I bought one. No, I never used it. I wanted purely platonic fuck-buddies. No, I never had any.

"I love your fishnets," she said enthusiastically, giving my Magenta getup the once-over.

I wore fishnet stockings then with no more chic than I can pull off now. Some girls are born to wear fishnets and others are not. Meg could have, but she wore an ancient pair of Levis, patched in places with suede, calico and other artfully curated materials, Western boots, and a leather jacket. Meg's going-to-the-midnight-Grateful-Dead-documentary-with-two-platonic-fuck-buddies outfit out-styled my punk-bisexual-incestuous-housemaid costume by a mile.

I stuck with a generic profile thereafter: jeans, t-shirts, sweaters, A-line dresses and skirts in solid colors, preferably black. No fishnets. No silver underwear, even under my jeans.

༄

—**Barbara A. Edelman** lives in Gardiner, New York (New Paltz's sushi- & bar-deficient neighbor) where she divides her days between working as a research editor and letting the dog in and out. She spends her nights sleeping and not sleeping. Mainly not.

Visit her at www.barbedelman.com or www.inyourownwords.biz

Kim Ellis

KIM ELLIS

Circles

We have been circling around each other like vultures.
We have been circling above the body of the Us.
The words we use are circles that return to the starting place.
We say: but the house, the roof, the boiler, the bank.
And beside speaking in circles,
There are the circles of ripples as the taps drip water
To keep the pipes from freezing.
Circles of frost on the windows,
Circles of toothpaste in the bathroom sink.
We have been circling around each other like dogs
Looking for a place to lie down and rest
In a round nest of solitude.
The small circles are graceful:
Tea stains
And lentils
And cucumber slices.
Circles are in the refuse of easy, familiar words
About appointments, oil bills, and garbage day.
On serrated black wings
We circle in on the scent of decay,
Not knowing who will land first.

☙

Mother

The first time I tried to write
about my mother,
the words exploded like grenades
all over the white paper field.
Pieces of A's, D's, and T's,
dead blackbirds on snow.

The second time I tried to write
about my mother,
the pen skidded away
as if skating on ice,
slicing bruised chasms,
with swift, deadly water below.

The third time I tried to write
about my mother,
the pen dragged through drifts
of burning, windblown sand,
bleached bones of words unsaid,
questions unasked,
too hot to touch,
and too late,
too late,
too late.

Next Time

She walked out.
She walked to Peter's Neverland.
Nirvana was too far,
so she stepped along the Milky Way,
second star on the right
and straight on 'til morning.
If the directions to Nirvana
had been as easy,
she would have gone there.
Neverland had its good points,
flying, for one,
and the mermaids did great things
with hair.
In the end, Neverland was not much better
than the place she'd left.
All that fighting,
ethnic cleansing,
and always having to watch out for pirates
with poison cakes.
Nirvana would have been a better choice.
Maybe next time.

☙

—**Kim Ellis** is a certified writing group leader in the Amherst Writers and Artists method and a Teacher Consultant with the Hudson Valley Writing Project. Her writing has been published in *Hudson Valley Parent Magazine*, *Chronogram*, *The English Record*, and *Crossroads*, a union newsletter. Kim recently won first prize for children's poetry from *Children's Writer E-magazine*.

Jeanne-Marie Fleming

JEANNE-MARIE FLEMING

Seeking Balance

Bless me father,
I am forty-five years old
And it has been forty-five days since my last period

These are my sins:

I drink too much caffeine
I cook dinners for the kids that do not include vegetables
I worry obsessively
I procrastinate paying my bills
I curse
    Slipping more often lately in front of my children
I get pissed off easily
My house is messy
I am lazy

Oh, and I have a boyfriend whom I delight in

Forgive me God
For all this, God, have you put me into early menopause?

Patience thin
Ready to pounce
Retreating to my covers
With laptop and vino
Dirty dishes left on counter

While my teens shoot and kill each other on X-Box
Want to see no one
Want to break up with my lover

Self-diagnosis of PMDD in June
Premenstrual Dsyphoric Disorder
Disturbing label
For a scary feeling

Gynecologist recommends Prozac
Slightly relieved, but more ashamed
To admit
I can't handle

July now
Been on this shit for a month
Still no period
And now my hair is falling out
What the fuck?

Going off the drug

Need my hair— more than I need my sanity
Or at least as much
God, I am not sure that you will understand this but,
If I am going to spiral down, I want to look good on the way

Remember this, friends, when you check me into the psych ward
Remember to outfit me sharply on the day of my admittance
No matter what the circumstances, it is important to look good
Mom (Avon Lady from the big hair eighties) would back me up on this

Seriously — calling on women of infinite wisdom

What would you choose?
Would you give up your tresses to be less irritable?
(I do not have a single friend who would say yes)

Would you willingly gain 25 pounds to be a kinder human being?
I am way to vain for that
(I forgot, God, to confess this- vanity, surely a grave sin)

Would you give up your money for inner peace?
Oh Greed—more ungodliness

Half the month—euphoria
Jokes in the classroom
Energy flowing in my chakras
Tender hugs for my boys
Light hearted banter with my boyfriend
Plan meals for dinner parties
Sing sweet soulful songs

Ovulation—like an ax, strikes
PMDD returns

I drive too fast on the Taconic
Sleep restlessly on couch
Eat nachos for dinner

Hold tension in my neck
Hold grudges
Grind teeth in my sleep
Flip my oldest son the middle finger behind his back
I'm sorry God—I know you can see this

So this—is this the balance I am seeking

Unfair I say
Forty-five days no period. This is crap
Forty-five days and still waiting

Started the second half of my life on Saturday
Forty-five years old
Not waiting

Ready

Ready to balance out the second half with the first
Sins and all

Bless me father, I am doing my best

Oh and please Lord,

      Let me keep my hair.

            ನಿ

   —Jeanne-Marie Fleming is a writer, educator, and mother of three teenage boys. She would like to thank her fifth grade teacher, Miss Hohl, for inspiring her with a love of learning and a passion for writing. J.M. lives in the rural town of Poughquag, NY, which she fondly refers to as The Quag.

Allison B. Friedman

ALLISON B. FRIEDMAN

Pillow Talk

1. Fly Away Home

So this is the thing, she told him. I cannot live with a bird, even a bird with a designer name like Kiwi. And, since we are discussing this topic, I must say I really loathe that wise-ass talking toucan on the Fruit Loops box. But lest we digress, I repeat: I simply cannot live with a bird.

Be reasonable, he pleaded, we're sort of a package deal.

I know, she said, I am fully aware. Thus, you can fully appreciate the gravity of my aversion.

Kiwi is not your average bird, look, look how cute she is, she's practically a person, a very colorful, sort of tropical person who happens to eat seeds, you know, vegan, very modern.

No, she told him, I cannot live with a bird. And I will not give you an ultimatum, but please, feel free to take one if you like. Just this: I am simply telling you one of the very few things I know to be absolutely true: I cannot live with a bird.

Why? What has she done to you—for that matter, what egregious error, what crime has bird-dom committed that has imprinted you to such a degree that I fear there is practically no room for negotiation?

Go where you go, she intoned, now a dull monotone. I. Cannot. Live. With. A. Bird.

Please, humor me. I feel as though I am supposed to know this somehow, but I just cannot log on. A hint? A clue?

Tippi Hedren, she said. Blame Tippi Hedren.

Tippi Hedren was never, not once, not ever, no way, no how,

assaulted by a parrot! Be reasonable! Kiwi is in a cage. I could open the door and she wouldn't even want to get out. I'm not even sure she remembers that she can fly.

Worse still. She shook her head. I absolutely can't live with a really dumb bird. At least in Tippi Hedren's case they had an agenda.

This is absurd! Tippi Hedren gets pecked to death in a movie, and somehow, this lands on poor Kiwi? Are you crazy? He was getting agitated. It did not impact her in the least.

No birds, she said. Deal breaker.

DEAL BREAKER? Are you serious right now? Our future hinges on Kiwi?

If you say so, she intoned. I can't have Tippi, or Kiwi for that matter, renting that much real estate in the area of my brain that I have allotted to the containment of my phobias.

You're phobic about Tippi Hedren, are you kidding me?

No, I'm phobic about birds in general. And, she said kindly, I don't think Kiwi should take it personally. It's more of a...pecking sort of thing.

But I love Kiwi! He was beginning to sound desperate.

Well then, she said, nothing should come between you.

I love you. This is madness! We can put her in the guest room.

No bird.

No bird?

No bird.

No you?

No me, no Tippi, no Kiwi, no Fruit Loops.

You drive a hard bargain. I love that about you.

I know, she told him, I know.

I already found a home for Kiwi, you know.

I know, she said, I know.

2. The Deading

Today, she told him, I have been thinking about killing my boss.
Really?
Really. All the live long fucking day.
Sounds cheerful.
Not so much, although I have been thinking about just how cheerful it would be to dead her, she said.
Dead her?
I forgot you don't do youth slang without interpretation. Dead her, cease to engage with her, confirm her irrelevance. Although as I think about it, actual deadness would probably be considerably more satisfying.
I am fearful that I lack the temerity to even ask what crime of the cubicle she has committed that has evoked your ire to such a disturbing degree. I mean, don't we hate her every day?
Indeed, she replied solemnly, we do.
He waited, arranging his face, feigning deep contemplative thought.
Stop feigning deep contemplative thought, she said. You know I hate it when you do that.
You hate that?
Well, yes, mostly, although I must admit there has been a time or two that I have found it kind of endearing.
He grinned.
This is not one of those times, she said. And now we are off-topic.
Tell me, he said. Tell me what she did.
She believes she really is the boss of me. She wants me to collude in that fantasy, which, as we have discussed, I find nearly impossible to do. It's a point of pride, you know.
I do know. She's got her nerve with that boss-dom thing. But can we get back to the deading part?

Oh, right. The deading. You will not believe this: She e-mailed me.

She e-mailed you?

She did. All capitals in the subject line, cyber-screaming. It was embarrassing,

What did it say?

It said: COME TO MY OFFICE. RIGHT NOW.

She scream-mailed you to come to her office? Isn't her office fifteen feet from yours?

Sixteen paces, actually, if you keep an even tempo, like Susan Sarandon in *Dead Man Walking*.

Did you go?

Of course I went. The fucking e-mail was flagged! Flagged!

She's unbelievable.

Right?

Right.

So I got up from my desk, and my knee collided with my open file drawer, ripping my favorite tights, the dark purple ones, the matte, not the shiny, you know them?

I know them, he said, instantly forgiving himself for not knowing them at all. A technical foul.

So now I am Dead Woman with Ripped Tights Walking the sixteen paces to her office, and when I get to her doorway, she doesn't even look up from her keyboard. She motions me in with that annoyed, exasperated gesture that says I really wish you weren't here, but come in if you must.

Bitch.

Yes. So there I am standing in my ripped purple tights in the middle of her office, awkward as hell. She's not even throwing me so much as a withering look, and I still have no idea what I'm doing there.

I can't stand it. I'm dying of suspense.

And this is what she says: Did I take my Ritalin today?

You have got to be kidding me.

I couldn't make this up if I tried. I was flummoxed. Completely flummoxed!

I doubt there are any guidelines in the Employee Handbook that cover the etiquette of this particular professional clusterfuck.

Right?

Right. Impressive set-up, he declared. No matter what you say, you will be wrong.

So this is what I said: The fact that I'm standing here in your office answering this question would suggest probably not. I was trying to be inoffensive! I even said, maybe your dose needs adjusting? Stop laughing.

I can't help it. Oh my God, this is incredible. If only Human Resources was on Nanny Cam.

Hah! I haven't even gotten to the worst part.

I'm steeling myself. I'm not sure I can take it.

Well, here it is. She finally looks up, hurls a spinning compass of evil right between my eyes, and then she says: Insubordinate! Get the hell out of my office! And don't show up for work again in ripped tights. It's unprofessional.

I'm dying!

You're dying? She's the one that needs deading.

Yes, my tender love, he said. Let's kill her together.

3. Hide and Seek

When you're angry with me, he told her, you become the Empress of Ice, reigning over Antarctic of Anger. You don't make it easy, you know.

Really?

Really. You disappear. You leave me clueless and freezing in the glacier of your emotions. Abandoned in the frozen tundra.

Are you going on the record with that?

No, why don't we keep it off the record? Then we won't find it necessary to include it in the Ledger of Unwinnable Arguments that you are keeping. I'm telling you, when you're enraged it's like you just…poof.

Poof?

Poof! Your body is still here, but the rest of you disappears without a clue. You don't even leave a trail of angry breadcrumbs.

That's ridiculous. Just because I'm mad at you doesn't mean I abandon you. I am not someone who lacks integrity, you jerk.

When you're really irate the integrity gets a little icy. Sort of random. Disorganized, even.

Disorganized? Really? Well, organize this. Here's a little story about integrity. Once upon a very short time I was a Junior Girl Scout. We were working on a Knitting Badge. Absurd. Knitting, knitting, endlessly knitting, and for what? For a sew-on patch embroidered with a ball of yarn with two knitting needles sticking out. Are you listening?

I'm pretty sure everyone in the building is listening, he said.

You're doing that eye-rolling thing. Don't push your luck. I could turn you to ice and poof at any time, you know.

Listening, eyes not rolling. Please continue.

The Knitting Badge. We all did it, a fucking troop of Girl Scout lemmings. Every one of us knitted a single, sad, lonely mitten. Mine was terrible, all lumpy, but it didn't matter. It resembled a mitten, and that's what counted.

What is the point of this irritating little tale?

The point is this: I knitted the fucking mitten, but I wouldn't take the badge. On principle. What is the value of one mitten? Mittens, by definition, are plural. Like people. Like couples, even when both parties are livid with one another.

How does this relate, even in the most tangential way, to the fact that you simply don't fight fair? How am I supposed to argue with the Queen of the Deep Freeze when you set me adrift on an island of ice without explanation? You don't even wave good-bye.

I don't fight fair? I offer no explanation? Right. You don't listen. You don't hear me. You don't even see me, apparently, except for my frozen breath. Now watch me, she said, and don't worry, you won't have to interpret anything. I am shaking my head.

When you're mad at me, I can't find you, he told her.

I know, she said sadly. But I dare you to every time, and you throw down and almost commit, but you get so scared and tangled up, like that grimy ball of mitten-yarn, that you forget where to look and what it is you're looking for. You can never find me, even when I'm hiding right here beside you, one mittened hand reaching for yours.

So that's where you are?

Maybe.

I always think you're leaving.

I know, she said. And forget the knitting badge. Sometimes I think I deserve a medal.

You're not leaving?

Stop! I'm here, and I'm definitely not leaving with only one mitten.

4. A Pregnant Pause

So get this, he said. Today I hailed a checkered cab, a really good one, vintage, the kind with the cavernous back seat and no shocks whatsoever.

We love those, she said.

Absolutely. On the back of the front seat, the horizontally uninterrupted kind, not buckets, there was a Mylar banner, silver and pink, sort of jaunty, the kind you'd find in the dollar store. "It's a Girl!" it said. It was sweet. Sort of unexpected, you know?

I know, she said. That is sweet.

So I said, "Hey, congratulations" to the back of the driver's head, and he told me something incredible, that he had delivered a baby girl, in the back seat of his cab last night. Right where I was sitting!

Yikes! Were you worried about your suit? I know how squeamish you can be.

Only for a second or two. It was unexpectedly thrilling, one of those iconic NYC stories people tell at cocktail parties. Anyway, the guy was so fucking proud, it was like it was his own kid or something. He said the mother was going to name the baby after him, but he didn't think that would really happen because it's not that easy to find a first name in Farsi that sounds good with the last name "Montgomery."

That's crazy!

It was crazy! He said it was such a miracle, seeing this baby emerge, right there on Central Park West, in the back seat of his cab, that he might have found religion, but he wasn't sure which one. And when I got out of the cab he gave me a Cuban, a really good one, which I almost refused because I know how you hate even the thought of the smell of it, but the guy insisted.

Well, she said, I hope you gave him a really big tip.

Fifty dollars on a $9.00 fare. But here's the thing: I keep thinking how I spend the day manipulating pretend money at lightning speed for people I don't even know, encouraging them to leave a sacrifice on the holy altar of Wall Street. But this taxi driver, he was like the patron Saint of the Checkered Cab. What he did was so real, so amazing, so extraordinary and ordinary all at once. I was humbled.

So, she said, are you saying that you want to have a baby or that you think it's possible that you could find enlightenment in a checkered cab?

It is uncanny, he said, how you can even read between the lines in my mind. I can't stop thinking about it, he said. It's like our theoretical someday suddenly morphed into now sounds good. A DNA merger, one with your eyes, although all things being equal, I would prefer her to be born in a manger that doesn't do double duty as a form of transportation.

Indeed, she said. And we're pregnant, by the way.

Don't make fun of me. I'm having a moment here.

I am too. And we are. Pregnant.

Hold on a minute, he said. I'm not sure I'm ready for this in real life.

They shared a very pregnant pause.

I guess that's why, she said kindly, this particular miracle takes a while to come to fruition.

I love you, he said. I love you both.

We love you, too. And I think a Farsi name might be just the thing. Our kind of holy, do you know?

5. Unbreak My Heart

Unbreak my heart, she told him. You do that, and I might believe you, or maybe not believe you, really, but I will cross the murderous abyss from here to there or somewhere else entirely, our destination to be determined solely by the timbre of your desires.

Crimes of the heart cannot be prosecuted, he said. And even it were possible, who would sit that jury? Six Montague's and six Capulet's? I never even meant to fall in love with you. I was only trying to toy with you.

Unbreak my heart, she insisted. She had surrendered her powers where he was concerned long, long ago; it was ancient history really. But the look on his face suggested he still didn't know it, so clever was the ruse.

I will it to be so, he said. I command your heart to restore itself. Now, say you love me.

She thought about it and decided not.

Say you love me, he said.

Unbreak my heart, she repeated. There are no more lines to be crossed; there are no clues left cleverly hidden, no ciphers unsolved, no further plausible theories to entertain. There is only this: the sticky yellow love line of police tape, meant to keep you at a reasonable distance, and it has failed to do so. You need to man up.

He was brooding, and she didn't need to look at him, she didn't even need to feel it, she could intuit him, that's how it always was, even when they were reaching for each other from opposing hemispheres. Just that way. Every time. Ancient. Perfect. Awful.

She was self-satisfied, he knew, doing that Cheshire cat thing she pulled out every so often just to make this love go extra-double-wide scary. He chose to pretend to ignore it. He knew that would get her attention. He hoped it would sear her to blistered.

A clever ruse, he thought for a nano of a nano-second before he remembered that this was no longer a game, it could even be a dress rehearsal, or the opening act of an actual farewell. Each time it seemed to grow more muddy, the murky sludge from the last round that much thicker, the sludge that was the choking of their breathless hearts. They held love like oxygen, deep within their lungs, each gasp foretelling the terrible exhale of a newly executed goodbye.

He was now breathing silence, in and then out, each breath the bellows of sudden fear.

No, he said. Unbreak my heart. It's your turn.

༄

—**Allison B. Friedman** is a writer, a practicing psychotherapist, and an active member of the Wallkill Valley Writers Workshop. In 2013, Allison's short story "Sahara Affair" was published in the award-winning anthology, *A Slant of Light: Contemporary Women Writers of the Hudson Valley*. In addition, she has published several short stories in literary journals, and wrote a newspaper column oxymoronically entitled "Understanding Adolescence" for the *Poughkeepsie Journal* for many years. Allison was a monthly columnist for *Living and Being* magazine, and a frequent contributor to the online Parent Resource Network. She was co-host and co-producer of "The Therapy Sisters," a live radio talk show in Kingston. Allison lives in New Paltz, NY with her husband, some or all of her four children, two dogs, and a malicious cat. She is currently at work on a novel, and has solemnly vowed that it will not defeat her.

Colleen Geraghty

COLLEEN GERAGHTY

Losing Time with Uncle Eddie

I wonder if some people are born filled up to their eyeballs with slime, or if they catch it while they are sliding out from between their mother's hairy legs.

Uncle Eddie was one of them slimy people who could stick to you like cement sticks to stones. I couldn't tell if he was born that way, or if he caught the slime from someplace else.

Standing in Grandmom's living room dusting his baby picture, it was hard for me to believe it was really Uncle Eddie tucked under the glass, smiling, his eyes shining like sunlight, every blessed thing about him black and white and clear as day. Somewhere along the road, he'd lost all his prettiness. And whether his ugliness built up inside of him before he was born, waiting to burst through the skin of his life, or whether his slime came from the outside like shit filling up a sewer, nobody but Uncle Eddie or God was probably ever gonna know for sure.

"It weren't no war that made Uncle Eddie mean," my big sister said. "Not like Uncle Rory or Uncle Billy. It was being double-crossed by God that turned Uncle Eddie sour."

"Being born a *kithogue's* bad enough on a person, but God cursing Uncle Eddie with a wandering eye too, that's what really made him mean," my cousin Marie added.

"What's a key-gog?" my little sister asked.

"A *key-tog*, you idiot," my big sister declared. "You know, a leftie."

"And you know what they say about lefties," My cousin Marie interrupted.

"They don't sit on the right-hand side of God," my cousin Bernadette added.

"With one eye wandering," Marie went on, "and the other one winking at the girls instead of looking at the chalkboard, the Sisters of Mercy tried to knock some sense into Uncle Eddie but...."

"They kicked him outa school in the fifth grade instead," my big sister butted in, "Sent him over to the Bricklayers Union where he's been ever since."

"It was them nuns at St. Stephen's that messed things up for my Dad. I know in my heart how it hurt him when they run him outa school, believe me, I know," my cousin Dee sulked.

"Leave it to the nuns to make a good thing bad," I said. "Look what they do to us every day."

"But I like Sister Anna," my little sister whined.

"But just wait, you'll get yours," Dee snapped, "Just wait, you'll get yours."

"Wait for what," my little sister asked.

"None of your damn beeswax," I interrupted. "Now, scram."

Cousin Dee and me knew what was waitin' on some kids. We knew how Uncle Eddie and his goddamn wandering eye could follow his wrong hand down the wrong road and end up sucking the good stuff outa the day. We knew how he had set to dry on us, how sometimes he stuck to Dee and me like stink on a skunk's ass, but we also knew how to keep our mouths shut and not go blabbing big girl stuff to a bunch of little kids. We were smart enough to know that some slimy shit belongs in big girls, and that little kids can't hear about it until they hang around Christ long enough to soak up enough holiness to be confirmed. At least with all that holiness, God might give a girl a chance at heaven instead of throwing her ass in limbo, purgatory or hell.

Sometimes so much slime let loose around here that I had to separate it and shove it into little boxes crammed up in my head:

one box labeled *the time before*, another box, *the time after*. And the worst crap, the stuff that hacked me near to splicing my own goddamn veins, I shoved into a box called, *the losing time*. I was smart enough to know that when really bad shit happens, some of us don't get back to the way we were before. Dee and me, we'd both been to *the losing time*. Her slime was a lot like mine so I knew she'd never get herself back to the way she was before.

It was kinda like the time Pop-pop sawed-off his ring finger. In *the time before* that saw hacked through his hand, his fingers had been solid around his whiskey cup, the gold of his wedding ring circled around his finger, just as his finger circled around the rim of his pipe. In *the time before*, his fingers were even happy wrapped around a sardine and onion sandwich. In *the time before* the hacking, Pop-pop could swear by all his fingers, but in *the time after*, in *the losing time*, the stub of his finger was nothing but blood and ooze. After that saw called on Pop-pop like Uncle Eddie came calling on Dee, nothing was ever the same. For anybody who's been to *the losing time*, nothing is ever the same.

Without a bunch of boxes in my head to cram shit into, my life woulda been hacked to pieces with worry. For Christ's sakes, I hoped my cousin Dee had found some boxes to fling her shit into before she went blabbing the truth about Uncle Eddie's nighttime sliming to a bunch of little kids who weren't big enough and holy enough to know what to do with it.

I hoped she wouldn't tell the little kids that sometimes slime comes for you at night, smothers you so hard that you lose yourself. You wake up in the morning, wash yourself real good, stare at your face in the mirror, even stick your tongue out, hold your eyelids back like you're pulling the shades off a window. You stare into yourself hard but you can't find who you were before. How do you tell the little kids about shit like that? How do you explain that you might look the same as *the time before* and everybody that sees you might think you're the same, but guess what? Once you've been through *the losing time*, you're just like Pop-pop's ghost finger.

I knew Dee had been to *the losing time*. I laid in the bed next to her listenin' to what God had waitin' on her—yeah, I mean God—that first night and all the other nights too. I heard Uncle Eddie stumble up the stairs, smelled his beer, cigarettes, his slime stinking up the bedroom as he opened the door and fell on Dee, heavy as a brick. The whole damn bedroom rocking while he sloshed and gurgled like wet cement, Dee laying under him like a dead whore, taking it all for her mother who was too tired to care—worn out, swollen in the belly with another brat.

After that first night, Dee knew that I knew a part of her had gone missing, but the next morning she never said a word to me. She crammed that *losing time* into some box in her head, I hoped, washed herself real good, and came down to breakfast like the rest of us. She sat there in *the after time*, across the table from her own goddamn mother. But my Aunt Issie was too busy serving up ham and eggs to Uncle Eddie to notice that Dee wasn't really there.

I watched Dee's eyes, saw her disappear like the sun behind a bustle of clouds, and I hoped she was looking for boxes, scrambling to find someplace she could cram all Uncle Eddie's goddamn slime. Chewing on my bacon, I knew how, being a good Catholic, she'd be forced to love him on account of him being her father. But he weren't no Dad to me! So, sitting there, sopping up the last bit of egg yolk with my toast, I looked at Uncle Eddie in all his slime and I decided to hate him.

I didn't give two flying shits when two days later Sister Maureen heard me holler, "I hate Uncle Eddie, pure and simple!" It didn't change me one bit to have her drag me off the schoolyard and force me to write a thousand times, "Hate is a sin. Thou shalt not hate." Sure, I wrote her stinkin' holy words till my own *kitoghue* of a wrong hand ached, but in my head, behind my eyes, in the darkest part of my heart, I cursed Uncle Eddie, Sister Maureen, and all that godforsaken slime.

As far as I was concerned, Sister Maureen didn't know slosh about slime, didn't know nothin' about cement. It was just like a nun not to wanna hear nothin' about nothin' that wasn't holy. How would she like it if she had to squish herself stiff as a corpse, night after night, her and her holy sisters squeezing their ass cheeks tight while the bed rocked, like Uncle Eddie was mixing cement and Dee was the trough he was mixing it in?

After living through one night of hell like that how would Sister Maureen like it if she had to sit around writing, "Hate is a sin, Thou shalt not hate"? So full of holiness she never bothered to ask me nothin' about hate, too full of heavenliness to know how close to hell Dee and me could get. How would Sister Maureen feel knowing some nights our bedroom was so slick with slime that all the boxes in my head and in God's holy heaven combined weren't big enough to shove all of Uncle Eddie into? Being a nun, she was probably too damn sinless to understand about *the after time*, too busy hollering about holy to know how to bury slime in a box or how the ghost of *the losing time* haunted me.

Maybe if Sister Maureen lived over on our crooked little street, she mighta had some mercy. Maybe if she'd been my real sister, she woulda known about Pop-pop's ghost finger, seen it when it came haunting Pop-pop while he was out in the garden piddling potatoes or hoeing. He'd rub the place where his finger used to be, the ghost of *the time before* reaching into *the time after*, skulking and moaning and itching its way through to *the losing time* haunting Pop-pop and all of us something fierce. Maybe if Sister Maureen let me tell her all that kinda shit instead of making me write, "Hate is a sin. Thou shalt not hate," she'd climb down off her sacred horse and find out how hate worked.

Instead of being my real sister though, she had me scrawling line after line of punishment across the page and wondering if Jesus hated his God, the Father, for pounding a couple of dozen nails into him on account of somebody else's sins too? Was Dee just like Jesus, loving her father in spite of his slime? What would Sister Maureen force me to write if I told her how me and my sister wore three pairs of underpants, even in the hot summer, or how when Uncle Eddie slimed his way into the bed, my big sister pulled me tight, and together we grabbed my little sisters and crammed their sleepy baby bellies up next to the wall so none of them got slimed? What would Sister Maureen make me write then, "Thou shalt not take the Lord's name in vain."?

"Hate is a sin. Thou shalt not hate," I scribbled over another page, and puzzled over whether God had already punished Uncle Eddie by giving him the wrong hand and a wandering eye. Had Uncle Eddie gotten up one morning, realized he was born in the *losing time* and so decided to be as spiteful as God and punish his golden-girl Dee?

"Hate is a sin. Thou shalt not hate," I wrote and wondered, if I was God, would I tell Dee to turn the other cheek? Would I holler, "I don't give a damn how you feel about slime, young lady, 'Honor thy father and mother.' "?

"Hate is a sin. Thou shalt not hate," I wrote, remembering the day we were out hanging diapers on the clothesline. A rough wind rolled beyond the trees and the ghost of Dee's *losing time* burst through the skin of her tongue and she flung her slime all over me. Pulling a clothespin out of her mouth, she shouted, "It don't bother me one bit, ya know. Ma's tired, and besides, he don't want no baby from me."

"Huh?" my big sister cried, looking like she'd been slapped.

"Hang the laundry, stupid," I shouted, reaching for another wet diaper and looking through the *losing time* at Dee.

While the wind took pieces of Dee's golden hair and tossed it around her face, we were quiet. I looked through her and caught sight of the wall Uncle Eddie was building brick by brick around Aunt Issie's garden. As I watched the wall circling around the summer flowers, I remembered that baby picture of Uncle Eddie, his smooth baby skin, cow-licked baby hair, thick baby lashes, a face as bright as an Easter lily. I stared at that wall and back to Dee. As she strung wet diapers in the bumpy wind, I wondered if Uncle Eddie ever had a *time before*, or even a *time after*, whether he was born filled up to his eyeballs with slime, or if he caught it when he was sliding out.

Either way, it didn't matter to me anymore. While I sat writing Sister Maureen's punishing, "Hate is a sin. Thou shalt not hate," I didn't care no more whether I figured out Uncle Eddie's *time before* or his *time after* cause as far as I was concerned, anytime with Uncle Eddie was *losing time*.

☙

—**Colleen Geraghty** is proud to be a member of Amherst Writers and Artists: Wallkill Valley Writers. Her stories have appeared in *Wallkill Valley Writers Anthology 2011* and in *Slant of Light: Contemporary Women Writers of the Hudson Valley*. Her short story, "The Beer House" was the first prize winner of the Hudson Valley Writers Guild 2013 Short Story Contest.

Kate Hymes

KATE HYMES

Sister Sojourner Testifies

The preacher finished – a woman's place
is in the pews and pulpit, his words
roiled over heads crowned in felt,
adorned with silk flowers and feathers.

A troubled noise disturbed the congregation
as spirit called forth
flesh. Black walnut fingers
laid hold the back of the pew
as her dry bones – no peace for the weary –
came together, rose with the breath
of the four winds full in her lungs
to testify one more time.

Preacher – Ain't I a woman. Ain't I
been called by God. Ain't I done
the Lord's work. Black, a woman,
a slave, can't read. I done heard
it all before.

Preacher – my master told me about the good
book. He say servant obey your master. He say
folks preaching abolition break God's
commandments – do not covet your neighbor's servant.
He say if I run away, I break another
commandment and I'm a thief – do not steal
a man's property. And he say freedom
against God's law. And I believed

until I met God for myself. In a clearing
in the woods, He snatched me
up into the middle of a July sun,
scared me so I prayed real hard.
Then Jesus came, stood between me
and that fearsome light. In that moment I filled
up with the word, felt like I would bust
wide open. I claimed myself. Became
truth. Let my tongue loose. Preacher – no man
can hinder me.

☙

Their Favorite Dish

Everybody gon be here.

Blue morning breeze encouraged
the gas flame to quick heat
a pot of coffee, to keep
hands and eyes alert
as the three sisters
sliced, diced, chopped:
onion, garlic, green peper, parsley.

Lillian won't come.

The news startled Florence,
The cooking oil heated
too hot, the roux burned.
She had to begin again, fresh
oil adding two cups of flour
little bit by little bit until
the roux looked and smelled
like roasted nuts.

She don't have no dish to bring.

Lucy scraped the seasonings
from the cutting board
into the pecan-colored paste. Tena
stirred and stirred the pot until
the onions went clear and limp,
while the heat made
the green bits shine bright.

Bernie coming though.

Florence filled the pot
to its brim with crab water,
then crabs followed by shrimp.
Lucy spiced the murky
liquid with bay leaf, thyme
and hot pepper. Tena set the lid
on top, confined the feisty brew
while time and a slow blaze
cooked it just right.

Every once and awhile
a splash of almost-ready
liquid boiled over, escaped
the bubbling pot, crusted
dry and hard onto the stove-top.
A combustible mix, the sisters simmered
in the midday sun.

They talked about Lillian, her three hungry babies:
how tired she looked,
how proud she was, even when
it came to her own family.

Too proud for her own damn good.

Then they talked about Bernie
who always showed up, rolled
right along with the good times:
ice-cold beer, hot food and raunchy music.

He got some damn nerve out having fun.

Florence propped the fan
on the windowsill. Its blades weighted down,
slow-churning with the grime of year upon year
boiling and frying to feed mens folk. Keep them
fat and happy. From the ice box, Tena
took three tall bottles of Falstaff
beer (they wouldn't drink that pissy stuff
called Dixie). They held the long-neck
bottles above the cleft of their breasts.
Let its cold sweat mix with their salt.

Gumbo done; the table set. The sisters still
boiled and bubbled; their heated dreams
stifled by a world of toil and trouble. More
than done with it all. They spilled into the alley
between the two shot-gun houses,
ambushed Bernie, whipped his narrow
ass, chased him home to
Lillian and her three precious babies.

༺༻

Believe

May you begin a new day
With abandon and passion
Hold within you the knowing
Wounds are possibilities
Made manifest at the edge-tip
Of scratchy pens and sharpened tongues.
May you believe the word
Your honest, brave words
Especially when your words rub
Against mine as coarse sandpaper
Wears down old patina to hard wood's
True grain – as a plow cuts earth, once frozen,
Now thawed – believe creating
A fresh field to ponder ready
For a new seed crop planted
Dirty hand in dirty hand
Sister-friend, brother-friend all of us
Wonderfully and fearfully made.

⁂

—**Kate Hymes** is reminded of the power of crafting stories and poetry every week in wVw writing workshops. The words of wVw writers have held and sustained her through a challenging year. She is more committed than ever to making it possible for anyone with the desire to use words to make art.

Barbara Taylor Martin

BARBARA TAYLOR MARTIN

Aunt Joyce

Aunt Joyce, the middle child of Grand-mama Bessie and Papa Joe, was my bestest aunt. When she came to visit, she had hugs and pats on the back for me. She was younger than Aunt Kate and Aunt Lucille, older than Uncle Roy and Ma. I thought she was prettier than all except my mother. Her short dark frame was plumper than her younger sister, Marge, my mother. No woman was as pretty to me as my Mom, especially with the deep dimples in her cheeks and sparkling white teeth when she laughed. But Aunt Joyce was pretty in her own way despite the numerous moles on her face and the forlorn air she carried most of the time. She allowed me to rummage through her handbag to find the stick of Juicy Fruit gum hidden there for me. She called me *peach pie*. I loved that. I felt all feminine and cute when Aunt Joyce called me *peach pie*.

I thought then that I was a good listener, but now that I am older, I'm not so sure. I remember half-heard conversations in Grand-mama's kitchen. Now I can surmise the significance of Aunt Joyce coming every day at five o'clock and whispering to Grand-mama. Sometimes I heard them talk about Buddy, Aunt Joyce's husband. Aunt Joyce sounded afraid and Grand-mama sounded angry. Both of them had stone cold eyes that barely softened when I asked, "What's the matter?" They never sat down, just stood in the kitchen with sad faces, as if they would like to run off to escape some monster.

Most of the time when she came to visit I heard those soft whispers. One particular night was different; there were only hugs and tears between Aunt Joyce and Grand-mama. Their voices hushed. I heard something about a hospital and what was Aunt Joyce to do. I started to cry too, even though I didn't know why, except that Grand-mamma and Aunt Joyce were very sad. After that night, I saw Aunt Joyce once more at her funeral.

I was in the yard jumping hop-scotch. Grand-mama started crying. Papa Joe went into his room alone. Lots of old ladies came to the house. Miss Bush, Miss Ross and Miss Williams, church ladies from across town, sat on the front porch with Miss Janie and Miss Beulah from the neighborhood. Miss Lettie, Miss Tommie and Aunt Money sat inside with Grand-mama. Never had so many people come. All the ladies cried. I hid under the porch to see if I could hear what all the visiting and crying was about. I heard them say that Aunt Lela was on the way because Aunt Joyce was dead. I wished I knew what dead was, but no one paid attention to me even when I came into the house. I sat quietly in a corner.

Even Aunt Joyce's husband, Buddy, came by and went into the room with Papa Joe. When Buddy came out of the room with Papa Joe, his face was ashy, swollen and sweaty, his eyes red and glazed over. He didn't speak, just walked out the back door toward Fronie Street where he lived with Aunt Joyce.

The next day one of Grand-mama's friend, whose cousin worked in the hospital, came by and told Grand-mama in a low voice, "Bessie, I heard she woke up during the operation and they rushed through it so fast they left some scissors in her." Grand-mama started to cry silently, and then folded her hands into her apron.

No one knows really what happened, but years later when my Mom had the same operation for fibroids, she didn't tell Grand-mama until it was over because of what happened to Aunt Joyce.

Now that I'm grown, I have started to piece together all that I remember. Grand-mama cussed about Aunt Joyce's husband until the day she died. He remarried shortly after Aunt Joyce died and started a family. Grand-mama said Aunt Joyce wanted children because she loved them so much, but she never had any. She never spoke to him after the day Aunt Joyce died, not even in church. She said he ought to be ashamed to show his face in public, especially in church, the way he mistreated her daughter and never complained about how the hospital let her die. Of course Grand-mama knew a black man couldn't complain about his wife's treatment in the south of 1954, but she still held him responsible.

೧

I Never Stop Seeing You There

Dear Grand-mama,

The sun was shining. I was packing, happy to be grown up and leaving that God-forsaken place. That house where I was born, grew up and love now, on that day, it held no future and no promise, just futility, anger, hurt and pain. Then I saw your face, the face that I had grown to know so well. That face had looked at me in so many ways for so many years, but never like this.

I remembered the sigh and frown that came from your scolding face when I had committed some small infraction that anyone else might have overlooked. All I did was to drop the bottle of milk you sent me to buy with your last fifty cents. I did not know that then. My ten-year-old mind felt that you made too big a deal of it by sending me to my room. I was glad that I didn't get a whipping. It wasn't my fault, because on the way home, the bad kids let their dogs out at me and I ran. I couldn't hold the milk and run. You were angry, so angry that I feared for my life.

Then there was the face I saw when I had the flu virus. I probably got sick because of our drafty old house and the chill got down into the marrow of my bones. Your mouth pursed, eyes gleamed with worry and anxiety as you rubbed Vicks salve all over my chest. You heated dreaded castor oil for my consumption. You said, "Cold castor oil makes you vomit. You got to keep it down for it to work." I pleaded with you not to give me the castor oil; I got it anyway. The orange juice you gave me afterwards did not take away the foul taste. Even warmed castor oil made me gag. The next day you forced a teaspoon of sugar soaked with turpentine down my throat to ease my cough. You gave me sassafras tea to sweat out the fever. I lost sight of your face as you cradled me in your size forty-two bosom. I was warm there.

I remember going to church and you told me, "Sit on the second row until the singing starts, then come sit by me." You were in the choir, so I didn't know which singing you meant. I kept hearing the choir sing, so I picked a song and came to sit by you in the choir stand. You frowned but didn't scold me while half the church wondered why I was sitting in the choir. I didn't realize until later that you meant I should join you at the end of service.

Your face glowed as you and Papa sat around the wood-burning heater and traded folk tales that made me laugh till I cried and I didn't want to go to bed. I remember the frowns in your angry face when Papa got up from the dinner table to go to the store and get my weenies 'cause I didn't like the squash you cooked. I saw pain and fear in your eyes when you brought Papa home from the hospital the day of his cancer surgery because he wasn't allowed to stay at the hospital and recuperate. I didn't see your face grieve on the day he died because the other women wouldn't let me into your room.

All of that is over, the sun was shining and I was leaving, leaving for a richer, more enlightened life in the big city with my Mom. You should have been relieved that you won't have to worry about me anymore. But there you were, sitting in that straight back chair, hands clasped tightly in your lap, tears streaming down your face, staring at my bags and saying, "Nobody needs me anymore."

ട്ട

—**Barbara Taylor Martin** was a native of Florida, and lived and wrote in upstate New York.

For Barbara

She only had to read a couple of lines and she had me or I should say that I had her forever in my heart. I didn't meet her that first time I heard her read but I knew that I adored her instantly, completely. She was the aunt I always had wanted and never had.

Months passed before I finally met this woman who had mesmerized me and captured my heart with her stories and spirit. On the two brief occasions we spent time together I was drawn to her as if she were a magnet and I, iron.

The last time I saw Barbara I had to tell her how I wished she were that aunt I always longed for. When she heard this she smiled that wonderful smile, her eyes twinkled and then we both laughed and ate some of her legendary pound cake.

Meg Dunne

Linda Melick

LINDA MELICK

The Alphabet Song

The children's scribbles run unruly
rivers round my eyes.
They show me double L's,
like collapsed strands of wool.
The S loops hold the eggs of an emu.
And the T with its fuss is a train track.
One hears the sound of the locomotive,
a beautiful O word.

The children clamor to climb on the train.
Their mouths make little A's as they hop on board.
Sometimes I sweep the hair off their necks,
sleek falling stiletto Z's and K's,
at times, runny Q's.
They cannot write yet, but they
sing the alphabet song
to the train tracks.

I hold their little hands and trace
their names on paper, over and over
loops and lines and extra go back to
cross the T, dot the I.
Their names stare back
at them, surprised and delighted.

The Eyes Have It

hawk eye, bright eye, no eye
in the kingdom of the eyes
the owl is the runner up

stoop down, pick yourself up
bend into a foreign form
freak out on your mother's
best doily

someone likes to sink
their teeth into porcelain teacups
spits out shards of glass

sweet Jesus winks one eye
at the thief on the cross
cases the joint himself
for a home invasion

fiscal, physical, ammonia can
killya don't know who
will come to mourn

Would You?

If your arthritis were crippling
you, would you be willing
to stick your head
in a beehive?
(As the Aztecs once advised)
The bees will swarm
and the honey will drip.
After a thousand stings
of random
penetration, you could be cured.

Would you be willing to lie
down on some sun-soaked
black top and roll your outside
body over tar? (like your great
Aunt Agnes) You will soak
up sticky covering on certain
sections. The pain would ease, such
a sweet release.

Would you be willing to give
yourself up and become
another person? A person
who was not blighted
with pain and did, in turn, cause
no pain. Could you shed
your selfishness as you cry
into your soup and become
that one
which you are not.

—**Linda Melick** has been writing poetry and prose for most of her life. She lives in New Paltz, New York. Her work has been published in *Green Fuse, Heavenbone, New York Writing, Todd Point Review* and other literary magazines.

Barry Menuez

BARRY MENUEZ

Chicago Style

In the autumn of 1958, Chicago was still the old tough Chicago. Mayor Richard J. Daley ran the city as the last powerful incarnation of the Irish-Catholic political machine. The city was racially divided and tense, with mass dislocations of poor folks, due to Daley's urban renewal destruction of block after block of aged apartment buildings. Whites fled to the suburbs as neighborhoods changed from white to black, the real estate blockbusters panicked whites into selling low. Bombings and fires were common assaults on the homes of black families moving in.

But I was happy to be there, living in a student apartment in the racially changing neighborhood of Hyde Park and two months into graduate work in Ethics and Sociology at the University of Chicago. With my pregnant wife MaryJane and our one-year-old son, Doug, I had moved there at the end of that summer after walking out of a career with the Harris Bank with only modest resources.

The previous spring I had met with the Dean of Students at the Divinity School of the University to explore possible admission. I was following a growing desire to heed an inner voice calling me to get serious about theological inquiry. After a long interview, I rose to leave, the Dean said, "We like people like you. Come in the fall and we'll work out the details."

He didn't care that my college efforts were just average and he was unimpressed by my two years as an officer in the US Air Force. I'll never know for sure what motivated him, but he arranged a full tuition scholarship, housing subsidy, a small fellowship and a requirement that I work for the University part time. I grabbed it, my lifeline to a new life. It was now or never.

One particular October afternoon stands out. I walked to my scholarship job as an orderly in the Emergency Room of Billings Hospital, the teaching hospital of the University's Medical School. I worked the four p.m. to midnight shift every Friday and Saturday. My route to work took me past Jimmy's Woodlawn Tap, the original home of the Compass Players and the launching pad for Mike Nichols and Elaine May, Shelly Berman and the Second City Theatre Company. I turned south onto Ellis Avenue and passed the haunting presence of the old stadium bleachers under which Enrico Fermi and his team of physicists produced the first sustained nuclear chain reaction, key effort of the Manhattan Project and essential to the production of the first atomic bombs, the ones dropped on Hiroshima and Nakasaki.

In the next block was the student bookstore and beyond that the first of many buildings of the Billings Hospital complex. Looking up, I could see the backside of the Roberts pediatric wing, a gothic mass rising ten stories above the bookstore. When I was seventeen, my father had brought me there as an emergency psychiatric patient suffering from a cluster of anxiety symptoms--all related to disruptive and chronic family dynamics. After an extensive interview and diagnostic workup, I was referred to a psychiatrist for several follow-up visits but was not admitted.

On my new job, I came to understand that all medical records, including mine, were in the basement below the emergency room.

My memory of this visit was so painful that I had kept it a secret. I had been holding my breath for years. I lied to the FBI about my past when they vetted me for a top secret/cryptographic clearance for my assignment with the Strategic Air Command. I had signed a statement declaring that I had never been hospitalized or treated for any mental illness or distress. I was still a captain in the reserves and if this falsification were discovered, I feared a court martial. Our country was just emerging from the toxic mindset of the Senator Joe McCarthy era. Apart from that hum of anxiety, I was really happy, infused with the promise and expectancy of this new life, free from the banking industry, free from suburban and commuter living. On regular class days, simply walking through the university quadrangle gave me a rush, a charge of energy.

I reported for work as usual that afternoon. The waiting room was relatively quiet at four P.M.; the real action came later on Saturday nights. My supervisor had me type up some intake forms. We used electric typewriters, recording everything on paper, computers still years away. By nine o'clock, the place was jumping: gunshot wounds, car accident victims, stabbings, emergency deliveries, broken arms, heart attacks, an infinite variety of illnesses and wounds.

By my second Saturday night on the job, I had begun to understand the system. Triage assessment by a medical team before admittance, usually while patients were still in ambulances; the medical team discriminated admissions by race. Black patients, if they were not bleeding out and close to death, were refused admission and sent off to the public Cook County Hospital. Others were victims of discrimination as well: alcoholics going into DT's, poor women--white or black--about to give birth, the poor, faint from high fevers, or screaming in pain from broken limbs. "Keep moving", was the staff attitude, and the off-duty Chicago cops who worked hospital security discouraged debate. This Saturday night the ER got wild; I was on the move chasing files, pushing patients on gurneys to x-ray, fetching coffee for the nurses, anything they thought I could do.

Near the end of my shift, I saw an old man unloaded from an ambulance being treated like a VIP. My supervisor, anxious to expedite the intake, called me over. "Here's the keypad security number for the medical records storeroom in the basement. Go down there and get Mr. Anderson's file. He's a University Trustee and big time donor!"

"But I've never been down there!" I said.

"Just go, goddam it. You'll figure it out," he said. "Go to the locator card file first, get his file number so you can go to the right cabinet and pull his folder. Bring it to me. Now!"

I ran to the elevator and got to the basement quickly. I punched in the security number. The door opened, then closed behind me. There I was, alone in this vast warehouse of four-drawer-high filing cabinets. Signs hanging from the ceiling identified the sections and rows. Suddenly, I was seized with an irresistible urge. With heart pounding, I raced through the maze of filing cabinets until I came to the one with the locator cards. I found the 3"x5" locator card that would lead me to the cabinet with my psychiatric file. Using the code from the locator card, I found my medical records. I pulled my folder and tore out the title page along with the diagnostic summary pages. I folded and stuffed the pages inside my shirt along with the locator card.

Remembering old Mr. Anderson still on a gurney upstairs, I moved as fast I could to find and extract his files and get back upstairs.

"Where the hell have you been?" asked my boss.

"It's confusing. I had to figure it out, did the best I could."

"OK, we'll take care of Anderson. You keep moving, get this woman to X-ray and get right back!" I shot off like a crazed Keystone Kop.

I left the woman in the X-ray queue and raced to the men's

room. I peered under the stalls to be sure I was alone. Then I tore up the incriminating card and summary sheets, and flushed them down the toilet. I was too stressed to read the report. But I knew that my file was gone. Forever.

I was so intent on cleaning up this old business that I hadn't weighed the consequences. Had I been discovered stealing and destroying medical files, a most serious breach of trust, the scholarship and all the rest would have been snatched away.

As the evening progressed, I calmed down and my heart beat returned to normal. I was kept very busy trying to keep up with my emergency room duties, the suffering of Chicago needing all the help it could get on a Saturday night.

Did I feel l guilty? No. I believe my action was right for me at that time and place. I found a name for my actions in my new graduate studies: Situational Ethics.

༜

—**Barry Menuez** is now in his sixth year with Wallkill Valley Writers, and believes that this community has given him support and encouragement to shape memory and experience into stories. He is retired from a long career in community organizing and urban/rural development programs.

RoseMarie Navarra

ROSEMARIE NAVARRA

Moving Day

Weeks of packing, clearing out closets and cupboards, sorting through books and papers and photographs, running garage sales, giving away so many things- the busyness of moving after twenty-three years of living comes to the moment when the house is at last empty and the truck is pulling away. I walk the rooms, wondering how long I'll be able to remember them— the rooms that had become for us places of comfort, of usefulness, of welcome and warmth and safety and love. Empty now.

My life with Jake started here. In this bedroom we made plans, made love, had fights, made each other laugh and cry and came to accept who we were. In this room I cared for him when he was sick and watched him weaken, helpless to stop it. Here I received the call in the night that he had died in the hospital. Here I sat on the bed not knowing what to do, what to feel, how to believe he was gone. This is not a room I'll forget.

I wandered around the house after that call, looking at each room, trying to remember every moment I'd had with him: every time he bounded up the stairs with a new idea, every time he sat devouring a persimmon, or working a puzzle or writing notes in his shirt-pocket notebook – every time he read to me from his writing or sang me Russian songs. I knew that night that no space in this house would ever be the same.

I had wanted to move away because the life I'd had here was over. But now, as the truck pulls out of the driveway and down the street, I think I was wrong. I'm not finished with it – there are still moments I want to remember, places I want to stand in, walks in the garden I want to take, mornings on the back porch I want to sit with my coffee. Everywhere here I can feel him, see his face, remember his voice, his walk, his way of folding the paper, gulping his boiling hot tea, messing up the kitchen with his cooking... melting my heart with his dopey grin.

℘

Look At Me

Look at me once more with eyes I used to know,
    as the child first sees an owl turn its head around,
    as the old man sees eighty candles burning on a cake,
    as the newborn holds its gaze, not knowing what you are.

I walk the house: make order, make clean, make food.
    I see my image as I pass the cloth over the mirror.
    I wonder what you see as I pass before you.
    I know you do not see me as before.

You look at me
    as when walking by, the woman glances at storefronts,
    as when napping, the old dog barely lifts its head to watch,
    as when sated, one looks askant at food.

I used to be the owl,
    the object of newborn gaze,
    the shimmering cake aglow.
Oh, look at me just one more time with eyes I used to know.

Upside Down

No one can see me trembling; it's internal. It's entropic. Everything falls apart from the center, like my Christmas pineapple upside-down cake, beautiful to see; only I knew the center had not held, that the middle pineapple ring has sunk lower than the rest, that the cherry in the center had disappeared into the batter.

Can't I make a pineapple upside-down cake anymore? Has that gone the way of my grasp on the world, on my beliefs, once so firm, on my sense of myself, my understanding of what my life has been, has meant? Everything, everything, jiggles in the center: the gelatin that somehow hardened only along the periphery, the Christmas lasagna that drooped sadly in the center.

It's the center, always the center, that doesn't hold.

The center of the body, the push and pull of the heart, distributing blood, oxygen, nutrients: all the years it went on, unnoticed, unheralded, working its job, moving with perfect rhythm, the elements essential for life, the center of the life of the body. And the center held! It held for three quarters of a century, and no one appreciated the miracle that was. Not until it didn't.

Last Spring, after years and years of glorious, fragrant blossoms, last spring, the hydrangea didn't bloom. It grew, filled out with bright green leaves, and then was struck still. Something in its center couldn't, one more time, push through. It looked ashamed sitting there, its leaves barely rustling in the breeze. Nothing could help it; it just couldn't bloom. I consoled it, forgave it, told it to believe in next year, told myself to believe in my own next year. But I wasn't convincing, not for the hydrangea, not for myself. Something in the center knew better.

Could I have put the upside-down cake back in the oven? Maybe another five minutes at three hundred-fifty degrees was all it needed. But no, we knew better, the cake and I. Its center had its time to hold, to gather heat and rise up. And my heart, shocked back to natural rhythm twice, knew what I knew: No! It had its seventy-five years of getting it right. All the electric shocks, the combinations of medications, the doses and treatments, the measurements and consultations – all, all, well-intended, carefully followed and charted, all with reprieves, no more solid than the fallen pineapple upside-down cake.

So what to do when the cake falls, when the lasagna sinks in the center, when the hydrangea can't bloom, when the heart, broken too many times, can't hold the beat? What to do?

෴

—**RoseMarie Navarra** was born in Beacon, New York before Beacon was a cool place to live: before plays were ever seen there, before there were antique or coffee shops, or galleries, or arts centers, before there was a Clearwater or a Pete Seeger, or a museum down by the River. But old Beacon did have a high-school English teacher named Miss Forrestal, who, when Rose was in her ninth-grade class, told her she was a writer. And sure enough, fifty years later, she began to believe her.

Jennifer Roy

JENNIFER ROY

A Cake for Pig Iron

The following excerpt is from a novel-in-progress. The work is based upon the lives of an African-American family who lived in a small, Illinois, coal-mining village at the turn of the twentieth century. Sarah, our protagonist, has recently suffered two losses: her husband's, Eldridge, death in a mine explosion and the revelation of her dearest secret to everyone of the town. A widow and an outcast, Sarah has to find a way to move forward and care for her infant son. In this excerpt she has re-married, but Eldridge's death still haunts her.

Fog draped itself like the most luxurious lilac velvet over the raw, jutting remains of corn stalks in the field. Sarah's feet found a furrow and she walked ahead, the ground obscured below her waist. She appeared to float across the field until she stumbled, which was often. She seemed to disappear entirely, only to emerge from the haze stooped over and dusting off her dress.

George Woods lived about a half mile northeast of the drainage ditch behind Carbon Hill. Sarah had baked two, heavy little pound cakes; one sat upon the kitchen table awaiting the return of her husband, Dandridge, and the other was nestled in the pail at her side, protected from all the jostling by a couple of dishtowels she'd taken off the line yesterday.

She rehearsed her greeting as she walked, "George, I wanted to thank you for your kindness at Bonucci's the other day. I'm pleased to have made your acquaintance." She couldn't bring herself to call George Woods, Pig Iron, like the town folk did. She practiced extending her hand with the pail to the man she imagined standing in the imaginary doorway.

When Sarah arrived at the Woods' property and found no one about, she was puzzled. A lantern hung on an upturned rake near a gaping maw in the ground. This must be his mine. She looked around for witnesses to her apprehension. She hesitated, "George, I brought you a cake!" she yelled into the dark chasm. "George! Mr. Woods?" she hollered.

"No need to yell little lady, I may look old but my hearing's jus' fine," Woods smiled a crooked smile.

Sarah blushed as she turned to the man standing behind her. She thrust the pail at him and repeated, as she stared at the dirt filled cuffs of his overalls, "I brought you a cake."

"Well, thank you Missy. Mighty nice of you to walk all the way out here to bring a feller a cake. Ain't seen many sweets since my Ruby left."

Swallowing the shock of his abrupt appearance, she fidgeted with her apron now that her hands were empty. "Could I see it?" she blurted out.

"What's that now?" Woods was genuinely puzzled and his head tilted a little like a terrier's.

"Could I see the mine?"

"Well, now, I never had any lady make such a request. We're a superstitious lot, us miners. Some men'll skip the day's wages if they so much as pass a woman on the way to work, let alone see one at the mine opening. What is it you want to see, exactly, Miss?"

"I want to know the darkness. My husband died in the mines a month ago, now. He was a shot firer. I just lost him to the earth. The men wouldn't let me see him. Just boxed him up and sent him back in the dirt. I just feel like I ought to know," Sarah said, barely meeting the man's eyes.

Woods made an audible sigh. "Aw, to hell with black cats and upside down horse shoes. Folk already think me a fool for bein' out here on my own why not add *Lady down the mine* to their list o' talk-abouts?"

He walked the cake into his modest, grey home and returned with a child-sized lantern. He lifted the hurricane lamp, which appeared delicate in his large, rough hands, lit the wick, settled the glass back into its holder and handed it over to Sarah. He reached for the larger lamp hanging from the rake and said, "Well, stay close behind me now and watch your head. You'll have to stoop down and it's hard to tell when. You might want to keep one hand in front of your head."

Sarah nodded as the man and his overalls turned toward the mine. The light from Mr. Woods' lantern projected out in all directions, distorting the jutting and withdrawn walls of earth. Sarah's own small light lit ahead of her to find George, doubly illuminating him like the conjoined, pale circles of a silver birch tree seed. She lifted her hand to an inch or so above her forehead, as if shielding her eyes from the sun, and was surprised when her hand thumped against a timber running across the ceiling. She had been watching Woods' boots and hadn't noticed his stooped gate.

The narrowness of the pathway had spun her senses as if through a funnel and she thought she could feel the earth breathe. There was, most certainly, a wind. Hairs on her arms stood alert as the air moved past her, the way a pale spider web trembles at the approach of something too big for the catching. She heard each of Woods' footsteps and her own, the fall of dirt from their soles and the scratch of the trail each time his right foot met the tramped ground. Her ears filled, overcome with the remnants of everything which had fallen from sight. The tunnel jogged to the left and Sarah lost the light of the mine's entrance behind her. Suddenly the lamp in her hand felt so inadequate. George was whistling a clear and full, summery tune that cut the chill and eased the steady jittering that had begun beneath Sarah's skin.

A turn again, her hand on the damp earth above signaled a further stoop was necessary. Hunched over, knees rising to her chest one after the other, she followed this whistling stranger into the dark. The path meandered organically. Clearly, George was not the boss of the mine; Mother Nature was simply letting him visit for a time. Silence.

Sarah stepped close on George, "This is as far as you're coming Missy. I couldn't live with myself knowing your knees were sullied by this business. You want wait here. I've got about twenty yards to go. I'll be 'round a few bends and you won't see me, or the lamp. I've got a shot I set up earlier and it's set to fire. If you'd like, you can sit here in the dark and listen. I hope you understand I can't have you near the firing." Sarah nodded and sat, crossing her legs within her dirtied skirt.

She cut the light of her lantern and watched the sway of George's halo until it disappeared and left her to the riotous sound of her own breathing. It seemed as if forever passed there in the darkness. She saw Eldridge in the dark there, pictured his face as real as can be. A smile. An explosion. And silence, thick as blood.

Sarah's eyes opened wide but found no light. A dark smell whirled into her nostrils and a gust of dirty wind floated her hair from her face. The air settled and she could again hear her heart beat against the tiny membranes in her ears. She felt grit on her face and tasted iron in her mouth. She must have bitten her lip when the shot fired. She swallowed the metallic liquid, and swallowed again to try to rid herself of the taste. She closed her eyes and let the world recede.

When George returned, his touch startled her awake. "Hard work got you napping Missy?" he chuckled. Sarah smiled sheepishly and followed him as he passed. The way up seemed shorter, the light, lighter.

༄

— **Jennifer Roy** has been a Wallkill Valley Writer for three years and enjoys researching and writing historical fiction. She is currently working on a novel about the lives of a biracial couple, who sought work in the Illinois coal mines at the turn of the twentieth century. She has been a secondary English teacher for 18 years. Her undergraduate work was done at the University of Arizona, she completed her Masters at SUNY New Paltz, and did post-graduate work at Teachers College, Columbia. Currently, she lives in Illinois and has plans to travel, write, and work on her art journals.

ACKNOWLEDGEMENTS

This has been a long and challenging year for **Wallkill Valley Writers**. First and foremost, I thank every writer in this volume who has exhibited extraordinary grace and patience throughout the year.

All my love to Bill Flanagan for keeping wVw writers well-fed and happy even as he struggled through the most difficult year of his life.

I am grateful for the love, support, understanding, well-wishes and so much more the wVw community has extended to the Flanagan family.

Thank you to Catharine Clarke, Soul Garden Press (soulgardenpress.com), for producing another beautiful volume to house our words.

Thank you to Claudia Battaglia, Tim Brennan, and RoseMarie Narvarra for opening their homes to wVw weekly workshops.

A special thank you to Claudia Battaglia for taking on the challenging job of serving as anthology copyeditor. Your keen eye was much appreciated.

Thank you to G. Steve Jordan, Jordan Gallery, www.mohonkimages.com, for cover artwork.

wVw is grateful for the support of Barner Books: Featuring new, used, out-of-print, and rare books. Barner also offers a large selection of handmade journals, and the legendary Blackwing Pencil. Located in the heart of New Paltz and online at www.barnerbooks.com.

FOR MORE INFORMATION

Wallkill Valley Writers (wVw) offers a variety of opportunities for writers, or others who wish to claim writing as their art, to write in a creative and supportive community.

wVw weekly workshop series. Eight to ten workshop meetings provide regular writing practice where writers develop and explore themes, stories, characters, genres and forms. Through the discipline of the workshop, writers devote a minimum of 40 minutes per week to their writing practice. Weekly workshop series take place in the New Paltz area. Schedule and registration online at www.wallkillvalleywriters.com.

Write Saturdays. For writers who cannot commit to weekly meetings, a Write Saturday provides the opportunity to devote a whole day (5-6 hours) to writing practice. Write Saturdays can be hosted in a number of locations. Contact Kate Hymes, khymes@wallkillvalleywriters.com, if you or a writing group is interested in hosting a Write Saturday. Schedule and registration online at www.wallkillvalleywriters.com.

Annual Writing Retreat. An extended multi-day writing in community including workshop sessions, private conferences and manuscript reviews. Retreats may include guest speakers. Schedule and registration online at www.wallkillvalleywriters.com.

Private Conferences. One-on-one writing conferences, and manuscript reading and critiques with Kate Hymes, khymes@wallkillvalleywriters.com.

Online Writing Community. Anyone interested in writers, writing or sharing stories can sign-up and join wVw online community. The work wVw writers will be featured on the web site, so you may continue enjoying the work of the writers in this volume, as well as other writers in the wVw community. You will receive news of wVw events and activities, readings, publications, recognitions, etc.

The back issue of **wVw Anthology 2011** and additional copies of **wVw Anthology 2015** may be purchased through www.wallkillvalleywriters.com, by contacting khymes@wallkillvalleywriters.com, or online at e-retailers.

CPSIA information can be obtained
at www.ICGtesting.com
Printed in the USA
FFOW02n0158190615
14413FF